MW00574363

Italian
Snacking

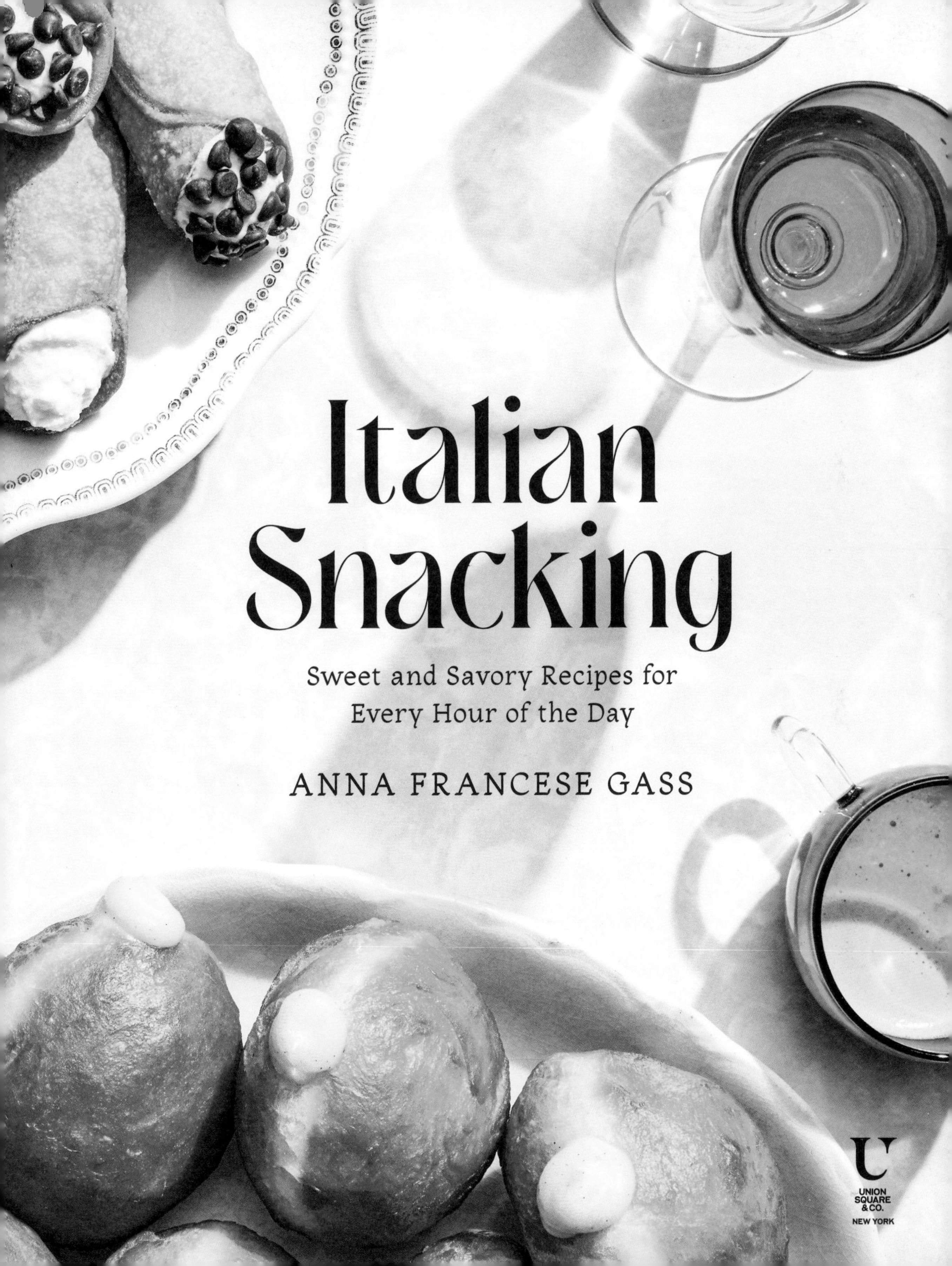

Italian Snacking

Sweet and Savory Recipes for Every Hour of the Day

ANNA FRANCESE GASS

UNION SQUARE & CO.
NEW YORK

UNION SQUARE & CO. and the distinctive Union Square & Co. logo are trademarks of Sterling Publishing Co., Inc.

Union Square & Co., LLC, is a subsidiary of Sterling Publishing Co., Inc.

ISBN 978-1-4549-4975-6
ISBN 978-1-4549-4976-3 (e-book)

For information about custom editions, special sales, and premium purchases, please contact specialsales@unionsquareandco.com.

Printed in China

10 9 8 7 6 5 4 3 2 1

unionsquareandco.com

COVER AND INTERIOR DESIGN BY Laura Palese
COVER ART BY Linda Xiao (front; back right) and Andrea Di Lorenzo (back left)
EDITOR: Caitlin Leffel
FOOD STYLIST: Greg Lofts
PROP STYLIST: Maeve Sheridan
ART DIRECTOR: Renée Bollier
PHOTOGRAPHY DIRECTOR: Jennifer Halper
PROJECT EDITOR: Ivy McFadden
PRODUCTION MANAGER: Kevin Iwano
COPY EDITOR: Terry Deal
PUBLICISTS: Blanca Oliviery and Kim Yorio

FOR MY DAD, WHO TAUGHT ME THAT THE
SKY'S THE LIMIT AND, MOST IMPORTANT, THAT NOTHING
IS BETTER THAN BEING ITALIAN

♣

CHAPTER 1

Spuntini di Metà Mattina

Midmorning Snacks
27

CHAPTER 2

Merenda

Afternoon Treats
75

CHAPTER 3

Aperitivi & Antipasti

Evening Appetizers
153

CHAPTER 4

Cibo della Strada

Street Food
199

WHAT ARE SPUNTINI?

WELL, it's the Italian word for "snacks"! *Spuntini* is an adorable Italian word that is fun (and easy) to say because it (sort of) rhymes with *martini*. Quite appropriate, as many spuntini are enjoyed with a delicious aperitivo.

Spunto translates as "quick" and/or "fast," and *-ini*, when attached to the end of a word in Italian, means "small." For example, *pane* means "bread," so panini are "little breads," or those rolls we fill with goodies and transform into sandwiches. Italians use the word *spuntini* in everyday conversation to reference an informal meal, something quick and small. Quite simply, a snack.

This book explores over a hundred spuntini, representing all the small meals Italians eat every day, and sometimes on special occasions. They are a joy to make and carry big flavor. They don't take long to consume, either—they're small bites designed to hold you over until the next main meal. They may be quick to consume, but that doesn't mean they are "fast food." While eating these delicious snacks, Italians relax, chat, and recharge while sharing the day's happenings with family and friends.

Combining simplicity and creativity, Italian recipes swirl together products like high-quality olive oil, salumi, cheese, and bread to create an unforgettable gastronomic experience. While I appreciate all of Italy's delicious culinary creations, I've found that it's the snackable, one- or two-bite meals that I obsess over the most. Hence, this cookbook dives into all the ways Italians snack their way through the day—and, sometimes, late into the night—so that taste buds are tantalized, get-togethers are filled with food and drink, and no one shows up to dinner starving.

Italians have undoubtedly mastered the art of the snack; crowd-pleasing bites can be found from tip to toe in the land of the boot.

Whether it's their *fritti*—breads, vegetables, rice, and even pastas, fried to perfection—or their crostini—where delicious bread becomes a vehicle for unforgettable spreads—Italians pull out all the stops when it comes to these between-meal bites. Even their not-too-sweet desserts make for a midmorning snack with cappuccino or the perfect afternoon bite. *Italian Snacking* will dive into the whens, whys, and *wheres* of these scrumptious snacks, providing a full picture of their role in Italian gastronomy.

The intersection of food and tradition is central to Italian culture—and plays a significant role in Italians' appreciation of heritage, familial respect, and observance of religious holidays. Mealtimes are never haphazard; rather, they're filled with meaning. Italians follow a specific schedule to remain satiated throughout the day, careful to avoid stunting the appetite by eating too close to the next meal. With that in mind, spuntini are timed to create a rhythm with the day's larger meals, so as to never spoil the appetite.

While I spent my childhood in the United States, most of my family was—and still is—in Italy. Growing up, I often returned to our homeland and, thus, became intimately familiar with its gastronomy. My sharpest childhood memories emanate from my nonna Grazia's Calabrian kitchen. She had this beautiful outdoor oven just steps from her front door, which she used to make countless delicious creations. As a young girl visiting, I thought this oven was magical. Made of cement blocks and ceramic tile with a stone lining, it was used just as much as the kitchen. Nonna would get up early and fill the back of the oven with branches collected from her vast garden. My sister and I, excited to participate, would follow her around as she picked the pieces that would soon be set ablaze. She would spend the rest of the morning kneading, chopping, and preparing food while periodically checking the oven's temperature. Last but by no means least, the special snacks—like *taralli* or bread rolls—would go in, perfectly proofed. Once done, she would reach in with a big wooden pallet and pull them out, golden and with the perfect crunch. Inside, she would prepare peperonata and slice up her homemade soppressata and cheese to produce the most exquisite antipasto platter. Meanwhile, my grandfather would water down some wine for my sister and me to sip while we giggled and ate from this special hearth.

Back in the States, our family home in Rhode Island was structured around the traditions and cooking practices of where we came from because, well, that is all my mother knew. Eating was never simply about sustenance. For Italians, sharing a meal is a ritual in which the entire family regularly participates. Instead of spontaneous snacking, these small meals were as reliable as breakfast, lunch, and dinner.

Italian snacks come in many forms, but their purpose is universal. Chefs and home cooks alike prepare these dishes with a few goals in mind: quality over quantity (true for all Italian food), light (even when fried), not too sweet (if it's a dessert), and, finally, enjoyable in just a few bites.

The snack foods of Italy, as with most of the county's dishes, are often connected to a particular region. Each region of Italy has a distinctive identity, not only in terms of architecture and culture, but also gastronomy. In the north, the dishes are hearty, "stick to your ribs," and rich with butter and cream; they draw from French, Austrian, and German influences in order to compensate for the cold winters. Head south and you'll find Greek, African, and Arab influences, in methods and ingredients. The coastline on both sides of this special peninsula boasts small-plate fish dishes—either fried or drenched in olive oil—for the perfect bite. Depending on where your travels take you in Italy, the gastronomic experience will be tied to the people, culture, climate, and geography. Each bite tells a region's particular story.

Italians structure their eating differently than Americans do. Spuntini are eaten at approximately the same time each day to prevent overeating at *pranzo* (lunch) and *cena* (dinner). Snacks are consumed to maintain a high energy level and an active metabolic rate throughout the day. While someone might not participate in every snack time every day, most will partake in a few for health maintenance, conviviality, and the prevention of a *buco nello stomaco* (an empty stomach; literally, a "hole in the stomach"). These small, flavor-packed bites are eaten either seated with family or at a local bar with friends. In Italy, each bite is to be savored and enjoyed with intention. Ingredients are pieced together with purpose, with the goal of simplicity and maximum flavor. I have thus arranged the snack foods here into four categories based on the time of day at which they are enjoyed: SPUNTINI DI METÀ MATTINA (midmorning snack), MERENDA (after-school snack), APERITIVI & ANTIPASTI (predinner snack), and CIBO DELLA STRADA (foods enjoyed in the streets, at any time of day, but often late at night).

SPUNTINI DI METÀ MATTINA

This small meal is the first snack time of the day. Usually a few hours after *colazione* (breakfast), it is a quick bite, sometimes as simple as a few pieces of cheese and salumi with bread, some chocolate, or even a light, sweet dessert. Most desserts in Italy are not heavy or laden with sugar and frosting; eating "desserts" midmorning or late afternoon is not considered odd or unhealthy. While Americans reserve desserts for after dinner or special occasions, Italians utilize simple desserts to stave off hunger until pranzo. The *pasticcerie* will still be bustling around 10 a.m., after the early-morning rush, with customers coming in for a cappuccino and a *cannolo* or *budino di riso*.

MERENDA

Merenda is widely known as an after-school snack for children. In many parts of Italy, however, it is also enjoyed by laborers after a long day of work. It is typically prepared at home, usually something simple or, if you are lucky, a dessert, such as a crostata or *ciambella*, left over from last night's dinner. Merenda is a light afternoon snack to eat while doing homework and telling your nonna (who graciously has it waiting for you when you walk through the door) all about your day.

The word derives from the Latin *merere*, meaning "the things one deserves." Home from school or hard labor, the idea is that a sweet treat or a small panino is needed as a reward for the day's work. Served usually between three and four in the afternoon, merenda breaks up the afternoon and guarantees you will make it to dinner without getting too hungry. Many Italians do not sit down for dinner until 8 or 9 p.m.!

APERITIVI & ANTIPASTI

Aperitivi is the time small bites and cocktails (also called aperitivi) are meant to be eaten, when the restaurants are closed and prepping for dinner service. It fills the time between finishing work and eating dinner and is enjoyed by university students, adults working from home all day, and those who want to break up the late afternoon before heading home after work. It also allows for social time with friends and coworkers. I call it the "Adult Merenda." It closely resembles happy hour here in the States, except that food is ALWAYS served! This snack consists of a traditional spritz or cocktail or glass of wine accompanied by spuntini. Italians do not usually drink to excess, using these delicious bites to absorb the alcohol and ensure a nice night out. Many spuntini can also serve as antipasti. Antipasti are the appetizer course of a dinner and are based on the restaurant or region; these snacks are interchangeable in many settings. In addition, this small bites and drink time with friends will often replace dinner for the younger crowd and is referred to as *apericena*, and after a night of entertainment, the group may find an after-hours spot to grab another delicious snack. This need for "party food" leads me to my final snack category . . .

CIBO DELLA STRADA

Just as in the States, *cibo della strada* (street food) can be used as a replacement for a more conventional meal. Street foods are usually available throughout the day and late at night. For example, you might eat street food when out partying with friends or celebrating at a festival or holiday. Street food is also incredibly popular with tourists who may not want to sit down at a restaurant and instead want to enjoy the beautiful sights of Italy. Peddlers have food stalls in heavily touristed areas for those curious to sample local specialties, but bars and bakeries also have many handheld delights for people to grab and take on their way; street food is both savory and sweet!

I have come to realize that while the delicious food I ate as a child nourished me, it also taught me about my origins. Growing up as an Italian profoundly shaped how I look at life, love, and tradition. What has become evident to me is that the day revolves around mealtimes in Italian culture. The rhythm of each day is dictated by the times we come together around a table for a large meal or for quick bites where you enjoy a pause from the hustle and bustle to rest, recharge, and check in with family and friends.

My hope is that this book, by highlighting the most special snack foods of Italy, will whet your appetite and help you to gain an understanding of the ingredients, flavors, and food traditions of each region. While you can make each snack whenever hunger strikes, I'll also show you how to pair a few to create a light dinner or a delicious spread for entertaining. In addition, the aperitivi here will allow you to get the true Italian experience.

La dolce vita—the sweet life—has become a common phrase, and it is a tried-and-true practice for Italians. It is indisputable that Italians value hard work, but their way of living is not focused on a fast-paced, "on the go" mentality. This book will show you how planned moments throughout the day dedicated to sitting, drinking, and enjoying food with friends and family produce a truly "sweet life." Everything revolves around family, with food at the center. Dive into this book of spuntini and learn to live like the Italians do, savoring la dolce vita.

I CIBI DELLE REGIONI

The Food of the Regions

ABRUZZO

For historical and economic reasons, Abruzzo is considered part of Southern Italy, as the dialect spoken is more similar to those of the south and the region's location is east of Rome. Within the region, the cuisine is diverse, and is distinct from that of the other provinces. In fact, Italians often refer to Abruzzo in the plural (*gli Abruzzi*). It has a mountainous inland and a beautiful coastline to the east, on the Adriatic, facing the former Yugoslavia. As a result, both meat and fish play a large part in its unique cuisine. Hence, with its history of shepherding, one of the most famous street foods is *arrosticini* where thin wooden skewers are threaded with thinly sliced lamb, simply dressed with olive oil, salt, and pepper and roasted on a special grill called a *canalina*.

PUGLIA

Located in the far south of Italy, the "heel" of the boot, Puglia is where vegetarians may feel most at home. Intense sun and far-stretching plains make for ideal farmland. Many meals are vegetable-focused, so while they may include meat, many times the star of the dish is the local and seasonal fruits and vegetables: the Mediterranean diet. Puglia produces over 20 percent of Europe's olive oil, so extra-virgin olive oil is commonly used for cooking and drizzling liberally over hot dishes or a plate of raw vegetables. Olives are present in so many Pugliesi dishes, especially at snack time. The Pugliesi are also known for their olive oil–laden focaccia (page 112). The plentiful olives also pureed in their own oil to make a thick pâté as well, served on crostini. Vineyards are also plentiful, and the hot summer temperatures give full-bodied reds like primitivo and Nero di Troia their sugar content.

VAL TREBBIA
DG 066VJ

BASILICATA

The "instep" of the boot, this beautiful area faces the Ionian Sea on the south, with a port, Maratea, facing the Tyrrhenian Sea on the west, and the high mountains of the Pollino in between. It is known as mountainous and rugged as well as seafaring—it is a land caught between land and sea. In addition, Basilicata is renowned for its delicious, cured meats and cheeses. No charcuterie board would be complete without some products from this area. Horseradish, known in Italy as the "poor man's truffle" is also used in one of their favorite frittatas, the Rafanata (page 181), a simple egg-and-potato dish enjoyed in the afternoon with a plate of meat and cheeses.

CAMPANIA

Campania, directly north of Basilicata, with Apulia to its southeast, is known for its gulfs, islands, and city life. The street food culture of its capital city, Naples, proves you can fry almost anything. At the same time, the seafood dishes for which the region's islands (Amalfi, Capri, and Ischia, to name a few of the better known) are famous make for a varied diet. Lemons, grown widely in the area, play a role in both savory dishes and desserts, and, of course, are the base for limoncello. The snacks and desserts from this area of Italy are a gastronomic playground with delectable fried cheeses, pasta, and the most famous pizza in the world, the Margherita (page 227).

CALABRIA

The "toe" of the boot, Calabria has lengthy Tyrrhenian and Ionian coastlines with the Apennine Mountains dramatically rising up between them. Therefore, Calabrian cuisine embraces both meat and seafood dishes, according to local traditions. Calabria was colonized by the ancient Greeks before being conquered by the Roman Empire, so a Greek influence can be seen in some of the dishes. Inland areas are known for pork dishes, while seafood is enjoyed in towns on its shores. The cuisine has a notable Mediterranean influence: Dishes are rich and, quite often, spicy. Mushrooms, eggplants, and onions are very common in many recipes and the region's lengthy history of economic underdevelopment can be seen in Calabria's *cucina povera*: Preparations are very simple but also bold in flavor. Bread and cheese fillings fortify the abundant vegetables eaten throughout the day to stave off hunger.

EMILIA-ROMAGNA

This region is a mecca for foodies and for anyone who enjoys a varied, classic cuisine. Emilia-Romagna, the home of Bolognese sauce, prosciutto di Parma Modena's balsamic vinegar, and Lambrusco (the wine naturally pairs with Parmigiano Reggiano, another Emilia-Romagna native), is in the Po River valley, Italy's breadbasket. Mortadella, the most famous cured pork product, shows up in many bites, on top of pizza, and as the favorite filling for Piadina (page 116), the region's sandwich bread. Midway between Rome and Milan, the landscape is characterized by fertile plains. The Po's deltas, which spill into the Adriatic, are a seafood paradise.

FRIULI–VENEZIA GIULIA

Italy's northeast outpost borders both Austria (to the north) and Slovenia (to the east). Separated from the rest of Europe by the Julian Alps, it looks southward to the Adriatic Sea.

Because of its cultural, historical, and ethnic diversity—which is reflected in the food—Friuli is one of five autonomous Italian regions. Italian is the official language, but you can hear Friulan, Slovene, and German spoken when you visit. The dishes of this area, like Frico Morbido (page 178), a potato pancake stuffed with cheese, are heavily influenced by the region's Slavic and Venetian neighbors (the city of Venice, despite the name, is not in this region; it is in Veneto), making the cuisine a melting pot. Prosciutto di San Daniele is one of its most famous products, known inside and outside of Italy. Sweets include strudels and fried fruits adapted from Austria and seafood dishes from Trieste (the regional capital).

LAZIO

While most famously known as the home of Rome, the Caput Mundi ("Capital of the World," as residents of the Eternal City still call it), Lazio has mountains, lakes, beaches, medieval villages (*borghi* in Italian), and fertile farmlands where wine, fruit, and vegetables of the highest quality are grown. When outsiders think of the cuisine of Lazio, the street food of Rome—which is delicious and devoured by countless tourists every year—comes to mind. Roman Supplì al Telefono (page 211), handheld meat-and-sauce-filled rice balls, are fried throughout the city. But the Laziali also enjoy variations of dishes consumed in neighboring regions.

LIGURIA

This crescent-shaped province bends around the northernmost part of the Ligurian Sea, bringing together the Italian and French Rivieras, while inland, its hills rise and join with the Cottian Alps. Liguria's picturesque coastline is a string of small fishing villages like Cinque Terre, so the area's love of seafood should not come as a surprise. (Liguria is also home to Genoa, a historic port city.) The food is thus the product of the area's unique climate, which is characterized by temperate winds blowing in from the sea and is actually similar to the climate of regions much farther south. Basil, an herb that thrives in warmer climates and abounds in Genoa, is the foundation of pesto, one of the region's signature dishes. Inland, where historically irrigation was relatively scarce, chickpeas were a popular commodity and Ligurians over time acquired a reputation for using chickpea flour to make snacks, breads like focaccia, and pasta.

LOMBARDIA

Lombardia, the country's financial capital, is geographically diverse, ranging from quiet countryside to the highest Alps to bustling cities (such as Milan, an important fashion and publishing hub) and hamlets. It is also home to Italy's lake district, with over fifteen different lakes dotting the landscape. As you would expect, the cuisine is varied. We find quick, metro food in Milan, comfort foods out in the countryside, and a great variety of cheese and meats from the large cattle farms throughout the Po Valley. Because Lombardia is so far north of the "olive line" (where historically it ceases to be feasible, because of the climate, to cultivate olives), butter and cream are staple ingredients here, perhaps more so than in any other part of Italy as seen in their Miascia (page 34), a rich bread pudding.

LE MARCHE

The food of Le Marche, located in Central Italy just north of Abruzzo and bordering on the Adriatic, is influenced by its topography and climate and conditioned by the traditions of the Marchigiani. Its idyllic countryside enables both wineries and olive groves to flourish. Its olives and olive oils, especially the Ascolana variety (Ascoli Piceno is a provincial seat, in the southwest corner of the Marche), appear in many dishes like their Olive all'Ascolana (page 191), where they are stuffed with meat and fried. Not surprisingly, residents have a penchant for dishes fried in local olive oils.

MOLISE

Lying between the Apennine ridge and the Adriatic Sea, Molise is in South-Central Italy (Puglia and Campania form its southern border, Abruzzo is just to the north, and in the west it brushes against Lazio). The food of this region is rustic and hearty, with many dishes centered on pork and lamb. The Molise are famous for Pampanella (page 222), where racks of pork-rich bones are grilled with paprika and vinegar. The Molisano also transform the offal of the lamb, sheep, and goats who graze in the abundant mountainous areas into delicacies. Termoli, a city on the coast, is the source of fish that residents use for traditionally rustic preparations of fish stews and soups of cuttlefish and trout.

PIEMONTE

Piemonte (literally "foothills") forms the northwest edge of the boot, bordering France and Switzerland. As you would expect, the cuisine (like the local dialects) exhibits French influences, with wide use of butter instead of olive oil. The climate is perfect for the region's hazelnut and white truffle industries, which contribute to making the food of this region distinct and delicious. Torino is Italy's chocolate capital, so you will be hard-pressed to find a better cup of hot chocolate or Nutella-stuffed sweets.

SARDINIA

Italy's second-biggest island is in the heart of the Mediterranean, right below Corsica. Interestingly, although it is an island and has delicious seafood dishes like clams and shrimp, it is a haven for foodies looking for superior meats and cheeses. Stuffing rich bread with ground lamb, as they do with their well-known Panadas (page 122), makes for the perfect bite. The rough terrain of the inland areas is well suited to sheep farming, so many of the most delightful pecorino cheeses come from this area.

SICILY

Sicily is the largest island in the Mediterranean, situated southwest of the Italian peninsula, directly south of Sardinia, and is separated from Calabria by the Strait of Messina. Its southern shore is a stone's throw from Tunisia and Libya on the coast of Africa as well as the island of Malta. Its coastal areas are warm, especially when a hot summer wind (the scirocco) comes up from the Sahara, so warm-weather fruits and vegetables—such as eggplant, tomatoes, capers, and citrus—thrive and are integral components of the cuisine. Palermo could be considered the street food capital of the world with vendors making and selling handheld delicacies on every corner and in two large outdoor markets that operate daily. From Arancine (page 212), a saffron-and-meat-studded rice ball; to Sfincione (page 235), an onion-laden pizza; to Cannoli (page 147), the handheld snacks one can eat are endless and delicious.

Sicily—in ancient times and as late as the 1800s—was called Trinacria because of its triangular shape. Its lengthy coastline encloses an inland area that is quite mountainous. There are volcanoes—Mount Etna overlooks the Ionian Sea to the east—on the mainland and volcanic islands (the Eolian Islands) just to the north, which have their own unique soil. Raisins and saffron are also among the local produce and are considered staples by locals. In addition, its strategic geopolitical location has made it the subject of conquest through the centuries (Greek, Roman, Arab, Norman), and so Sicily's cuisine is a fusion of the influences of its past.

TRENTINO–ALTO ADIGE

This region embraces forestland, lakes, rivers, streams, vineyards, and apple orchards. The southeast border is formed by the Dolomite peaks, while the north is defined by the Alps. It is culturally heterogeneous; the south, Trentino, is ethnically Italian, whereas the official language of the Alto Adige was German until it was reassigned to Italy in the aftermath of the First World War. The cuisine in this part of Italy is therefore reminiscent of what one would expect to enjoy farther north in Europe. A perfect example is Kaiserschmarren (page 47), a dense pancake served with jam that was borrowed from their northern borders.

TUSCANY

Located in the heart of Italy, this centrally located region has something for everyone. The fertile plains are perfect for animal breeding (so beef products become more popular as we get up into the Apennines) and the coastline is a fish lover's paradise. Climate and topography vary throughout the region, making some areas ideal for wine production. Tuscans love enjoying a hearty red wine with a dish of creamy chicken liver pâté (Fegatini di Pollo, page 160) on top of some oil-drizzled crostini. In sum, the cuisine of Tuscany has a singular range and depth, allowing Tuscans—and us, with them—to enjoy it all.

UMBRIA

This region is smack at the center of the boot (Foligno, an ancient town in the province of Perugia, is nicknamed "Italy's belly button") and is the only region without any coastal access. Don't expect to find fresh seafood here! Over the centuries, Umbrians developed recipes for salted fish, such as *baccalà*. Umbria's terrain is a mix of plains, hills, and mountains. The Tiber runs through on its way to Rome, and Lake Trasimeno, the largest lake in central Italy, also appears in this region. Umbria is well known for its meat production, especially the salumi, and its skilled butchers. On the sweet side, it is also famous for its chocolate, with the Perugina chocolate factory in Perugia creating the world-famous Baci candy. Eating their high-quality chocolate, with a bit of bread or on its own, is a perfectly acceptable afternoon pleasure.

VALLE D'AOSTA

Located way up north, nestled between Piemonte, France, and Switzerland, the Valle d'Aosta is a skier's paradise. Monte Bianco (Mont Blanc), the highest peak in the Alps and in Western Europe, straddles the Aostan-French border. Mountain glaciers feed the streams that irrigate the region's ample fertile pastures and farmlands. The food is rich and hearty, characterized by a strong love for butter, rich sauces, thick puddings, and Swiss-style fondue called Fonduta (page 172).

VENETO

This region, in the northeast corner of the country, is home to one of Italy's most diverse cuisines due to its variety of landscapes. It includes the Po Valley, the Adriatic coastline, the Dolomite Mountains, and, of course, Venice. The cuisine varies from province to province. Coastal food is quite different not only from what you find in the mountains but even along Venice's bustling canals. Italians make the most of local ingredients and Veneto is no exception. For example, the *cicchetti* (think Italian tapas)—like Baccalà Mantecato (page 161), a whipped salt cod spread—eaten in the bars of Venice are very different from the rich stews served in the homes of Verona.

CHAPTER 1

SPUNTINI DI METÀ MATTINA

Midmorning Snacks

Pizza Ebraica

FRUIT CAKE BISCUITS

Several restaurants and bakeries celebrate Roman Jewish cuisine in the city's old Jewish quarter. The understated Boccione (there is no sign on the door) is the most revered. Everything they produce is rooted in history, and completely delicious. Their Crostata di Ricotta e Visciole (page 87) is one of my favorite desserts of all time. This "pizza"—really a sweet biscuit, soft on the inside but hard, crunchy, and almost burnt on the outside—is another of their popular offerings. (I add a little bit of cherry juice to the dough for extra sweetness.) In Rome, the lines outside the bakery to grab this iconic handheld biscuit (also called *pizza di Beridde*) usually disperse only when the bakery sells out.

MAKES
10 biscuits

¼ cup (62 grams) white wine

¼ cup (40 grams) raisins

1½ cups (145 grams) almond flour

1¾ cups (175 grams) 00 flour

¾ cup (165 grams) sugar

½ teaspoon kosher salt

1 cup (150 grams) candied fruit, minced

⅔ cup (80 grams) raw slivered almonds

⅔ cup (95 grams) raw pine nuts

¾ cup (150 grams) maraschino cherries, halved

1 teaspoon maraschino cherry juice

½ cup (109 grams) almond oil

- Preheat the oven to 400°F. Line a 9 × 13-inch baking sheet with parchment paper.
- In a small bowl, combine the wine and raisins. Set aside to allow the raisins to plump while you prepare the biscuits.
- In the bowl of a stand mixer fitted with the paddle attachment, combine both flours, the sugar, and the salt. Mix on low speed to combine, 1 to 2 minutes.
- With the mixer running, add the candied fruit, almonds, pine nuts, cherries, and cherry juice. Add the wine and the raisins. Add the almond oil, then raise the speed to medium-low and mix until all the ingredients are combined and the mix-ins are evenly distributed, 1 to 2 minutes. Transfer the mixture to the prepared baking sheet and press it into a 10 × 7-inch rectangle.
- Cut the rectangle into ten 2 × 3½-inch squares and arrange them ½ inch apart on the pan.
- Bake for 25 to 30 minutes, until the bottoms are almost burned and the tops are dark brown in spots. Transfer the biscuits to a wire rack to cool completely before serving.

◆

PANE FRITTO, DOLCE O SALATO

Fried Bread, Sweet or Savory

WHENEVER I have a crusty loaf getting a bit dry, I wake it up by transforming it into *pane fritto*. This recipe is essentially Italian French toast: Crusty bread is dropped into a liquid custard and fried until golden. But there are a few reasons I love these recipes more than the "French" version. First, there is both a sweet and a savory option. Depending on the mood, the custard can be made with milk and sugar or milk and cheese. And second, for the dolce, the recipe begins with simmered sweetened milk like my nonna used to make for me. I love the smell of warm milk and sugar, as it brings me right back to her Calabrian kitchen.

DOLCE, PAGE 32
SALATO, PAGE 33

PARMIGIAN
REGGIAN

Dolce

SERVES
2

- 2 cups whole milk
- ½ cup granulated sugar
- 2 large eggs
- 2 tablespoons extra-virgin olive oil
- 1 tablespoon unsalted butter, plus more for serving
- 4 (1½-inch-thick) slices crusty Italian bread (from ½ loaf)
- Confectioners' sugar, for dusting (optional)

◆ In a medium saucepan, whisk together the milk and granulated sugar. Bring to a simmer over low heat, whisking every 3 minutes, until the milk has reduced and thickened, about 30 minutes. It should remain white. Reduce the heat to very low if the milk begins to darken. Remove from the heat and let cool.

◆ In a large shallow dish, beat the eggs. Slowly drizzle in the cooled milk mixture while gently whisking to combine.

◆ In a large sauté pan or griddle, heat the olive oil and butter over medium heat. When the butter has melted, place the bread, one slice at a time, into the custard, flipping it to coat both sides, then place it in the pan. Working in batches if necessary, fry the bread for 2 minutes, until golden brown on the bottom, then flip and cook for 2 minutes more, until golden brown on the second side. Transfer to a serving dish and top each piece with a bit of butter. Dust with confectioners' sugar, if desired. Serve immediately.

Salato

SERVES
2

2 cups whole milk

½ cup finely grated Parmigiano Reggiano cheese, plus shaved cheese for serving

2 large eggs

2 tablespoons extra-virgin olive oil

1 tablespoon unsalted butter, plus more for serving

4 (1-inch-thick) slices crusty Italian bread (from ½ loaf)

¼ cup chopped fresh flat-leaf parsley, for garnish

- In a medium saucepan, whisk together the milk and cheese. Bring to a simmer over low heat, whisking until combined, about 5 minutes. Remove from the heat and let cool.

- In a large shallow dish, beat the eggs. Slowly drizzle in the cooled milk mixture while gently whisking to combine.

- In a large sauté pan or griddle, heat the olive oil and butter over medium heat. When the butter has melted, place the bread, one slice at a time, into the custard, flipping it to coat both sides, then place it in the pan. Working in batches if necessary, fry the bread for 2 minutes, until golden brown on the bottom, then flip and cook for 2 minutes more, until golden brown on the second side. Transfer to a serving dish and top each piece with a bit of butter. Sprinkle with the parsley and a few shavings of cheese and serve immediately.

Miascia

BREAD PUDDING

Miascia is a traditional bread and fruit cake from Lombardia. As Italians are known for never allowing anything to go to waste, this recipe is perfect for using up stale bread and fruit that may have seen better days. Apples, pears, and raisins are folded into custard-soaked bread and baked until golden on top. Garnished with rosemary and a dusting of confectioners' sugar, this bread might have humble origins; however, the result is anything but. I first tried this delicious snaking cake while staying on Lake Como, and I knew I needed to re-create it at home. Instead of a traditional cake pan, I love making it in a loaf pan, cutting it into hearty slices, and serving it with a dollop of whipped cream.

SERVES
6 to 8

- 2 tablespoons unsalted butter, melted, plus more for the pan
- ¼ cup raisins
- 3 to 4 tablespoons amaretto liqueur
- 4 large eggs
- 1 cup whole milk
- 1 cup heavy cream
- ¾ cup granulated sugar
- 2 teaspoons vanilla powder or pure vanilla extract
- 1 teaspoon kosher salt
- 1 medium loaf very stale bread (peasant bread is ideal), cut into 2-inch pieces (5 cups)
- 1 small apple, peeled and cored
- 1 medium pear, peeled and cored
- 3 tablespoons confectioners' sugar, for dusting
- 2 rosemary sprigs, for garnish

◆ Preheat the oven to 350°F and butter a 9 × 5-inch loaf pan.

◆ Place the raisins in a small bowl and pour the amaretto over them. Set aside to soak while you prepare the other ingredients.

◆ In a large bowl, whisk together the eggs, milk, cream, melted butter, granulated sugar, vanilla, and salt. Add the bread and press it into the custard, squeezing the bread to encourage absorption. Set aside.

◆ While the bread soaks in the custard, cut the apple and pear into small pieces (you should have about a cup of each). Fold the apple, pear, and soaked raisins (with their soaking liquid) into the bread mixture.

◆ Pour the bread mixture into the prepared loaf pan and, using a spatula, spread it evenly. Bake for 50 minutes, until the top is puffed and the sides are golden brown. Transfer the pan to a wire rack and let cool for 20 minutes before removing the bread from the pan to slice. Alternatively, the bread can be spooned out of the pan while still hot and served immediately. Dust with the confectioners' sugar and garnish with the rosemary before serving.

Strudel di Mele

APPLE STRUDEL

Apple strudel is one of the most popular autumn desserts of Trentino–Alto Adige. This dessert traces back to the Turkish domination of Hungary; the Hungarians tweaked a Turkish snack similar to baklava, where nuts and honey were wrapped in a thin pastry, to its current form, which incorporates fruit. As a result, it is enjoyed throughout Austria and Northern Italy. Trentino–Alto Adige has a few different versions, with each kitchen personalizing the dough and the filling. Some prepare it with Austrian-style dough that is rolled so thin, you can see your knuckles through it, while others roll out a more rustic shortbread crust. Rum raisins and pine nuts are very common additions, along with a bit of cinnamon for a spiced filling to adorn the golden apples grown in the region.

I decided to simplify the process by using store-bought puff pastry. It gives the strudel a flaky, buttery crust. For the filling, I added ground shortbread cookies to soak up the rum and apple juices. This recipe makes two beautiful strudels (the puff pastry comes in a pack of two sheets), so why not make one now and freeze the other for a rainy-day snack?

MAKES
2 strudels

½ cup (80 grams) raisins

3 ounces rum

10 or 11 shortbread cookies, like Walker's or Lorna Doone

1 cup (113 grams) pine nuts

3 large Golden Delicious apples (about 1½ pounds), peeled, cored, and cut into ¼-inch dice (about 4 cups)

Zest and juice of 1 lemon (2 teaspoons zest and 3 tablespoons juice)

2 teaspoons ground cinnamon

½ cup (100 grams) granulated sugar

1 teaspoon kosher salt

1 (17-ounce) package frozen puff pastry, preferably all-butter, thawed

1 large egg, beaten with 1 tablespoon water, for egg wash

Confectioners' sugar, for dusting

- Preheat the oven to 375°F.
- In a small bowl, combine the raisins and rum. Set aside while you prepare the filling.
- In a food processor, pulse the cookies until they are the consistency of fine sand. Process enough cookies to yield 1 cup.
- Scatter the pine nuts on a rimmed baking sheet and toast in the oven until shiny and nutty, about 5 minutes. Set aside to cool.
- In a large bowl, combine the apples, lemon zest, lemon juice, cinnamon, granulated sugar, salt, toasted pine nuts, and ground cookies. Drain the raisins, discarding the rum, then add them to the mixture.

RECIPE CONTINUES

- Unfold 1 sheet of puff pastry on a lightly floured piece of parchment paper. Use a rolling pin to lengthen the pastry sheet into a 9 × 13-inch rectangle. Place the parchment with the pastry sheet on a baking sheet. Spoon half the apple mixture down the middle of the pastry. Leave a 1-inch border at each short end. On an angle, cut six slits about 2 inches apart down each of the outer sides.

- Beginning with one outer side, lay one diagonal strip across the filling, then repeat with a strip from the other side. Continue folding the strips, creating a diagonal braid all the way down the center. Fold the top and bottom borders over the filling and press to seal. Brush the top with the egg wash. Repeat the process with the remaining puff pastry sheet, filling, and egg wash to make the second strudel.

- Bake for about 40 minutes, until the pastry is golden brown and the apples are fork-tender.

- Set the strudel, still on the baking sheet, on a wire rack to cool for 20 minutes. Once cooled, dust with confectioners' sugar and cut crosswise into 8 to 10 slices.

STRUDEL DI MELE,
PAGE 37

STRUDEL DI FUNGHI E
MASCARPONE, PAGE 40

Strudel di Funghi e Mascarpone

MUSHROOM STRUDEL

In Trentino–Alto Adige, mushrooms are cultivated and foraged. The mushrooms found throughout the region have been revered since ancient times and referred to by the ancient Romans as the food of the gods. Found both in cultivation caves and out in the woods growing wild, the bounty lends itself to various uses. Simple buttons, trumpets, morels, chanterelles, and even porcini are found in the woodlands and used in many dishes.

Borrowing from German-Austrian cuisine, strudels celebrate the farms' ingredients. This buttery lattice dough enrobes these mushrooms, herbs, and speck, the most common cured ham of Alto Adige. If you can source some for this recipe, it adds a bit of smokiness, as it's part of the curing process. However, prosciutto can be substituted, if needed. I love to assemble all three strudels, bake one for immediate snacking, and save two in the freezer for when friends pop by for a glass of wine before dinner.

MAKES
three 3 × 13-inch strudels

DOUGH

¾ cup (171 grams) warm whole milk (110°F)

1 teaspoon active dry yeast

½ teaspoon sugar

3¾ cups (540 grams) 00 flour

½ teaspoon kosher salt

1¾ sticks (141 grams) unsalted butter, cut into pieces, at room temperature

1 large egg

1 large egg yolk

FILLING

3 pounds white button mushrooms, thinly sliced

3 tablespoons extra-virgin olive oil

1 large white onion, finely chopped (2½ cups)

1 teaspoon kosher salt

1 teaspoon freshly cracked black pepper

1 cup chopped (¼-inch dice) speck

1 cup mascarpone cheese

TOPPING

1 large egg, beaten with 1 tablespoon water, for egg wash

1 tablespoon chopped fresh rosemary

1 tablespoon flaky sea salt

◆ MAKE THE DOUGH: In a small bowl, stir together the milk, yeast, and sugar and let stand for 10 minutes.

◆ In the bowl of a stand mixer fitted with the dough hook, combine the flour, salt, and butter. Add the whole egg, egg yolk, and milk mixture. Mix on low speed until a soft dough forms. Transfer the dough to a lightly floured work surface and roll it into a large ball. Cover the dough with plastic wrap and refrigerate for 30 minutes.

◆ MEANWHILE, MAKE THE FILLING: In a large sauté pan, cook the mushrooms over medium heat, stirring occasionally, until they turn brown and have released most of their moisture and the bottom of the pan is dry, 15 to 20 minutes. Stir in the oil, onion, salt, and pepper and cook until the onion is soft and translucent, 5 to 7 minutes. Add the speck and stir to combine. Remove from the heat and stir in the mascarpone until it melts and coats the mushrooms. Set aside to cool while you ready the dough.

◆ Preheat the oven to 375°F.

◆ TO ASSEMBLE: Weigh the dough ball and divide it into three equal portions. Wrap two portions and return them to the refrigerator.

◆ Place the remaining portion of dough on a floured sheet of parchment paper and roll it into a 9 × 13-inch rectangle.

◆ With a short end facing you, score the dough lightly into three equal parts, each about 3 inches wide. Be careful not to completely cut through the dough. On an angle, cut thin strips (about ½ inch wide) down the left and right sides of the dough. Take one-third of the filling (about 2 cups) and spread it down the center of the dough. Fold one strip from the left side over the filling, then repeat on the right side, overlapping the first folded strip slightly. Continue folding strips over the center, alternating sides, all the way to the bottom. Fold the top and bottom ends over the filling and press to seal. Brush the top with egg wash and sprinkle all over with one-third of the rosemary and flaky salt. Repeat with the remaining dough, filling, egg wash, and topping.

◆ If you're baking the three strudels at once, line two baking sheets with parchment paper and place two strudels on one sheet, 3 inches apart, and the third strudel on the second sheet. Position racks in the upper and lower thirds of the oven and place one baking sheet on each rack.

◆ Bake for 35 minutes, rotating the pans halfway through for an even bake, until the strudel is dark golden brown on the top, sides, and bottom. Transfer the baking sheets to wire racks and let the strudels cool for 15 minutes before serving.

Rocciata di Assisi

DRIED FRUIT AND NUT STRUDEL

This sweet, fruit-and-nut-filled strudel originated in the town of Assisi and is eaten throughout Umbria and Le Marche. Growing up, we made these for Thanksgiving because after making all the holiday pies, there was always one pie crust left over. We would roll it paper-thin and fill it with jam, chocolate, nuts, dried fruit, and cherries. To be honest, I preferred it to the pies. I have a lovely dough recipe here, but feel free to make it with prepackaged rolled doughs. As for the fillings, use my list as a starting point and swap in your favorite jams, fruits, and nuts. The only nonnegotiables for me, are, of course, the chocolate chips, which are not traditional at all but are always my favorite part of any sweet treat.

MAKES
two 5 × 12-inch strudels

DOUGH

2¾ cups (319 grams) 00 flour

1 teaspoon kosher salt

8 tablespoons (113 grams) cold unsalted butter, cut into 8 pieces

1 tablespoon extra-virgin olive oil

½ cup cold water

FILLING

2 cups fig jam

2 teaspoons ground cinnamon

1 cup mini chocolate chips

1 cup dried figs, cut into small pieces

½ cup raisins

½ cup chopped walnuts, toasted

10 to 12 Amarena cherries, halved and pitted

1 large egg, beaten with 1 tablespoon water, for egg wash (optional)

Raw or sanding sugar, for sprinkling (optional)

• MAKE THE DOUGH: Pulse the flour and salt in a food processor to combine. With the motor running, add the butter, one piece at a time, then slowly stream in the olive oil. Slowly add the water and process until the dough comes together; you may not need all the water. (Alternatively, in a large bowl, combine the flour and salt. Add the butter and work it into the flour mixture until the butter breaks down into very small pieces. Slowly add the oil and mix to combine. While kneading the dough, slowly add a few splashes of water, incorporating all the loose flour.)

• Transfer the dough to a floured work surface, divide it in half, and knead each piece into a soft ball. Cover with plastic wrap and refrigerate for 30 minutes.

• Preheat the oven to 350°F.

• On a 9 × 13-inch piece of parchment paper, roll out one ball of dough into a very large oval, about 10 inches wide and 12½ inches long, almost to the edges of the parchment. Transfer the dough on the parchment paper to a baking sheet. Repeat with the second ball of dough.

• Divide the fig jam evenly between the rounds of dough and spread it over the surface of each, leaving a ½-inch border. Sprinkle the cinnamon evenly over the jam. Sprinkle the mini chocolate chips, figs, raisins, walnuts, and cherries evenly over the jam.

• Working with one strudel at a time, lift the parchment lengthwise to fold the two long sides of dough into the middle, creating a long roll. Press the edges together to seal. At this point, it is traditional to gently move the ends in to create a horseshoe shape. Brush with the egg wash and sprinkle with raw sugar, if desired. Repeat to form the second strudel.

• Bake for about 35 minutes, until the strudels are golden and the filling is bubbling. Set the baking sheet on a wire rack and let cool completely. To serve, cut each strudel crosswise into 10 to 12 slices.

Pasticciotto Leccese

CUSTARD AND CHERRY TARTLETS

My Calabrian aunts love to make *bocconotti*, muffins filled with various jams and Nutella, for their nieces and nephews. On one visit to the Amalfi coast in Naples, I was in a pastry shop and saw what I thought were bocconotti in the bakery case and had to order one. I took a bite and was delighted to find that instead of jam, this one was filled with vanilla custard cream with a few Amarena cherries hidden at the bottom of the muffin's interior. Here, it was called a *pasticciotto*, and I learned from the baker that the original version, which is from Lecce, Puglia, does not include the cherries. I love the Neapolitan version that includes the cherry, but if you can't find cherries or decide to go without them, you can enjoy the pasticciotto Leccese-style. Either way, these tartlets are decadent and are a perfect accompaniment for your morning cappuccino.

MAKES
19 tartlets

VANILLA CUSTARD FILLING

2 cups whole milk

4 large egg yolks

¾ cup granulated sugar

1 tablespoon vanilla paste or pure vanilla extract

2 tablespoons cornstarch

½ teaspoon fine sea salt

3 tablespoons cold unsalted butter, cut into pieces

DOUGH

4 cups (480 grams) all-purpose flour

1 cup (200 grams) granulated sugar

1 (16-gram) envelope lievito vanigliato (vanilla-flavored yeast), such as Bertolini or Paneangeli (see Note)

1 teaspoon vanilla powder or pure vanilla extract

1¼ cups unsalted butter, at room temperature, plus more for brushing

5 large eggs

16 Amarena cherries in syrup, such as Fabbri, drained (optional)

Confectioners' sugar, for dusting

RECIPE CONTINUES

◆ MAKE THE CUSTARD: In a large saucepan, heat the milk over medium heat until it begins to simmer, about 3 minutes, then remove it from the heat.

◆ In the bowl of a stand mixer fitted with the whisk attachment, beat the egg yolks, granulated sugar, vanilla, cornstarch, and salt on medium-high speed until light and fluffy, about 1 minute.

◆ Add a few splashes of the warmed milk to the egg mixture, beating the mixture to incorporate and ensuring the eggs do not scramble. With the motor running, slowly add the remaining milk to prevent the eggs from separating.

◆ Return the entire mixture to the saucepan and cook, whisking continuously, over medium-low heat, until the mixture resembles a loose pudding, 6 to 7 minutes. Stop whisking and let the custard bubble for a few seconds. Remove from the heat and add the butter, one piece at a time, whisking after each addition until smooth.

◆ Transfer the custard to a heatproof bowl and cover with plastic wrap, pressing it directly against the surface of the custard to prevent a skin from forming. Refrigerate the custard for 1 to 2 hours, until thoroughly chilled.

◆ MAKE THE DOUGH: Sift the flour and granulated sugar into a large bowl. Add the lievito vanigliato and vanilla and whisk to combine. Add the butter and 4 of the eggs and knead until a smooth, cohesive dough forms, 5 to 7 minutes. Cover the dough with a kitchen towel and let it rest for 10 to 15 minutes.

◆ Preheat the oven to 350°F. Generously brush 19 tartlet pans or muffin cups with butter.

◆ Pinch off a 1½-inch piece of dough (about 2 tablespoons) and roll it into a ball. Flatten the ball on the counter, then place it into a tartlet pan. Use your fingers to press it over the bottom and up the sides of the pan. Repeat 18 times.

◆ If using, place 1 Amarena cherry into each dough cup. Spoon 2 to 3 tablespoons of the custard on top (the dough cups should be filled almost to the top). Tap each tartlet pan on the counter a few times to level the custard.

◆ Pinch off another 1½-inch piece of dough (about 2 tablespoons), roll it into a ball, and flatten it on the counter. Place it on top of one of the custard-filled pans and pinch the edges of the dough together to seal in the filling. Repeat to top the remaining tartlets.

◆ Whisk the remaining egg with 1 tablespoon water, then brush the top of each tartlet with this egg wash. Bake for 20 to 25 minutes, until the tops are golden and beginning to crack in places.

◆ Transfer the tartlets in their pans to a wire rack and let cool completely before removing from the pans. Dust with confectioners' sugar before serving.

NOTE

You can stir together 2 teaspoons baking powder and 1 teaspoon vanilla powder as a substitute for the Italian vanilla-flavored yeast.

Kaiserschmarren

ORANGE-SCENTED PANCAKE WITH BLUEBERRY JAM

This delightful snack has Austrian origins and is enjoyed throughout Trentino–Alto Adige. It reminds me of a Dutch baby, but it's tastier and can be prepared solely on the stovetop. Perfect after a morning of skiing, this fluffy, orange-scented crepe is cut up into messy pieces and served with a jam "dipping sauce." Get creative and change up the mix-ins. For a boozy accent, try subbing in rum for the liqueur, but I love the flavor the orange liqueur adds. This recipe includes a blueberry jam that comes together quickly, but the pancakes also taste great on their own, with store-bought applesauce, or with a pat of butter.

SERVES
6

¼ cup raisins

3 tablespoons orange liqueur

6 large eggs

½ cup granulated sugar

1 teaspoon vanilla powder or pure vanilla extract

¼ teaspoon kosher salt

6 tablespoons unsalted butter

1 cup whole milk

Zest and juice of 1 orange (¼ cup juice)

1½ cups all-purpose flour

1 teaspoon neutral oil, such as canola or grapeseed

Confectioners' sugar, for serving

Simple Blueberry Jam (recipe follows), for serving

- Preheat the oven to 375°F.
- Place the raisins in a small bowl. Pour the liqueur over the raisins and allow to soak while you prepare the batter.
- Separate the eggs, placing the yolks in a large bowl and the whites in a medium bowl. Whisk the sugar, vanilla, and salt into the yolks until combined and pale yellow, 3 to 4 minutes.
- In a small saucepan, melt 2 tablespoons of the butter over medium heat (or melt the butter in a small bowl in the microwave). Whisk the melted butter and milk into the egg mixture. Add the orange zest and juice and whisk again to combine. Sift in the flour and mix until just combined.
- Using a handheld mixer, beat the egg whites until they form stiff peaks, 4 to 5 minutes. Drop one-quarter of the egg whites into the batter and mix to lighten. Gently fold the rest of the egg whites into the batter until just combined.
- In a large cast-iron skillet, combine the oil and 2 tablespoons of the butter and cook over medium heat, swirling the pan to coat the bottom as the butter melts, until the butter begins to brown.

RECIPE CONTINUES

◆ Scrape the batter into the skillet with the browned butter and shimmy the pan to smooth the top. Drain the raisins, reserving the liquid, and sprinkle the raisins over the top of the batter. Carefully drizzle the liqueur over the top as well.

◆ Place the skillet in the middle of the oven and bake for 20 minutes, until the top is puffed and golden and the middle is cooked through (a tester inserted into the center should come out clean).

◆ In a small skillet, melt the remaining 2 tablespoons butter over medium heat (or melt the butter in a small bowl in the microwave).

◆ To serve, scoop the Kaiserschmarren onto a large serving platter and cut it into jagged pieces. Brush the pieces with the melted butter and dust with confectioners' sugar. Serve immediately, with the blueberry jam.

SIMPLE BLUEBERRY JAM

MAKES 1 CUP

3 cups fresh or frozen blueberries
1 cup sugar
Zest and juice of 1 lemon
1 cinnamon stick

In a medium pot, combine all the ingredients and bring to a boil. Reduce the heat to medium and cook, stirring frequently, for 25 minutes.

Pour the jam into a bowl and serve with the Kaiserschmarren. Leftover jam can be stored in an airtight container in the refrigerator for up to 1 week.

Rustico Leccese

PUFF PASTRY PIZZA POCKETS

These handheld pockets are made all over Salento, on the "heel" of the boot. Sold in bars and small delis, this cheese-and-tomato-filled puff pastry is typically eaten while walking to work or school. These are simple to make and the perfect snack food, as they remind me of the Hot Pockets I used to eat as a child, but so much better, because of the crisp but buttery exterior and the creamy béchamel on the inside.

MAKES
12 pastries

1 (17-ounce) package frozen puff pastry, preferably all-butter, thawed

2 to 3 tablespoons all-purpose flour, for dusting

1 cup Béchamel (recipe follows)

1 cup Quick Marinara Sauce (see page 265) or Gina's Tomato Sauce (see page 264)

1 cup shredded low-moisture mozzarella cheese

2 teaspoons dried oregano

1 large egg, beaten with 1 tablespoon water, for egg wash

Kosher salt

- Preheat the oven to 400°F. Line two baking sheets with parchment paper.

- Place both puff pastry sheets on a lightly floured work surface. Roll them out until each pastry is very thin and approximately a 9 × 13-inch rectangle. (Sprinkle the top with flour if it begins to get sticky.) Using a 3-inch round cookie cutter, cut 24 rounds of puff pastry, 12 from each sheet. Place the rounds on the prepared baking sheets.

- Place a heaping teaspoon of the béchamel in the center of each round, leaving a ¼-inch border. Place a heaping teaspoon of marinara on top of the béchamel. Sprinkle a heaping teaspoon of shredded cheese on top of the sauce and a bit of dried oregano on top of the cheese.

- Place another pastry round on top of the filling. Using a smaller 2½-inch round cookie cutter, press down gently on the top pastry round to create an indentation around the edge and seal in the filling. Brush each round generously with egg wash. Using a fork, crimp the border created by the indentation all the way around, sealing the edges.

- Sprinkle salt on top of all the pastries. Bake for 15 to 18 minutes, until they are puffed and golden. Serve hot.

BÉCHAMEL

MAKES 1 CUP

2 tablespoons unsalted butter
2 tablespoons all-purpose flour
1¼ cups warm whole milk (110°F)
2 teaspoons freshly grated Parmigiano Reggiano cheese

In a heavy-bottomed medium saucepan, melt the butter over medium heat. Add the flour and whisk to create a paste. Cook for 2 minutes, until a medium-brown color is achieved.

Add the milk in a slow drizzle, whisking continuously until the sauce begins to thicken. When all the milk has been added, cook, whisking, until the béchamel coats the back of a spoon, 3 to 4 minutes. Add the cheese and mix to combine. Remove from the heat and let cool.

Once cooled, the béchamel can be stored in an airtight container in the refrigerator for up to 1 week.

Pizzette Delizia

SQUARE PIZZA POCKETS

This Sardinian puff pastry pizza is simple to make, delicious to eat, and so pretty to look at. You'll find them served in pastry shops and bars all over the island as a popular savory midmorning snack. Like the Rustico Leccese (page 50), these are puff pastry pizzas, but there's no need to make a béchamel for these, and they are square instead of round. After stuffing, the tops are scored, so as they puff in the oven, the filling begins to peek out from the center.

MAKES
9 pizzettes

2 to 3 tablespoons flour, for dusting

1 (17-ounce) package frozen puff pastry, preferably all-butter, thawed

1 cup Quick Marinara Sauce (see page 265) or Gina's Tomato Sauce (see page 264)

1 cup ½-inch cubes fresh mozzarella cheese

2 teaspoons dried oregano

1 large egg, beaten with 1 tablespoon water, for egg wash

Kosher salt

- Preheat the oven to 400°F. Line a baking sheet with parchment paper and sprinkle it with a bit of flour.

- Roll out each puff pastry sheet on a floured work surface until very thin and an approximately 9 × 13-inch rectangle. (Sprinkle the top with flour if it begins to get sticky while you are rolling it out.) Stack one sheet on top of the other. Cut the layered sheets into 9 equal squares. Remove the 9 top pieces and set aside.

- Spread 1 tablespoon of the marinara in a very thin later on each of the 9 bottom pieces. Sprinkle the mozzarella evenly all over the sauce. Sprinkle the oregano all over the mozzarella.

- Carefully top each pizzette with one of the reserved 9 pastry pieces. Cut six horizontal slits through the top of each pizzette, leaving a border around the edges. Press the edges with your fingertips to seal in the filling.

- Place the pizzettes at least ½ inch apart on the prepared baking sheet. Brush with the egg wash and sprinkle with salt. Bake for 15 to 20 minutes, until puffed and golden brown. Let cool for 5 minutes before serving.

Mattonella

HAM AND CHEESE PIZZA SANDWICH SQUARES

In Sicily, the variations of snack and street foods are endless. Many are created with a brioche dough, which we will explore, in depth, on pages 238–252. However, one snack I found (and loved) while visiting Palermo was mattonella. *Mattonella* means "small brick" in Italian, and much like the Pizzette Delizia (page 53), it is a puff pastry pocket baked on a large sheet pan and then cut into squares. However, in Sicily, instead of slits, the tops are adorned with sesame seeds. Also, in this version, ham is scattered inside to add a nice salty pork flavor to the pizza filling.

SERVES
9

1 tablespoon all-purpose flour, for dusting

1 (17-ounce) package frozen puff pastry, preferably all-butter, thawed

3 to 4 tablespoons Quick Marinara Sauce (see page 265) or Gina's Tomato Sauce (see page 264)

8 ounces fresh mozzarella cheese, cut into 1-inch cubes

4 ounces boiled deli ham, cut into small pieces

1 tablespoon dried oregano

1 large egg, beaten with 1 tablespoon water, for egg wash

2 tablespoons sesame seeds

- Preheat the oven to 400°F. Line a baking sheet with parchment paper.

- Sprinkle half the flour onto a work surface and roll 1 puff pastry sheet into a rectangle approximately 9 × 13 inches. Carefully lift the puff pastry onto the prepared baking sheet.

- Spread the tomato sauce evenly over the puff pastry. Dot the sauce with the mozzarella and evenly sprinkle the ham over the cheese. Sprinkle the oregano evenly over the ham and cheese.

- Sprinkle your work surface with the remaining flour and roll the second piece of puff pastry into a 9 × 13-inch rectangle. Place the pastry over the ham and cheese filling, line up the edges, and use a fork to seal the edges.

- Brush the egg wash evenly over the pastry, including over the sealed edges, then sprinkle the sesame seeds over the entire surface. Bake the mattonella for 20 minutes, until the pastry is puffed and golden brown on top. Let cool on the baking sheet for 20 minutes, then slice and serve immediately.

Pizza Parigina

PARISIAN PIZZA

This pizza is an interesting hybrid from Naples: The bottom is a traditional pizza dough, topped with sauce, cheese, and ham. But then a large sheet of puff pastry is laid on top to cover and it's baked until the bottom is crunchy, the middle is warm and melted, and the pastry is golden brown. The puff pastry, a French invention, is why Italians consider this a Parisian-style dish. Decadent and delicious, this pizza "sandwich" is a local favorite with many enjoying it any time of day.

MAKES
one 9 × 13-inch pizza

2 tablespoons extra-virgin olive oil

1 recipe All-Purpose Pizza Dough (see page 263)

3 cups Quick Marinara Sauce (see page 265) or Gina's Tomato Sauce (see page 264), or 1 (28-ounce) can crushed tomatoes

8 ounces sliced deli ham, cut into small squares

1 pound shredded low-moisture mozzarella or caciocavallo cheese

1 teaspoon kosher salt

1 teaspoon dried oregano

1 sheet frozen puff pastry, preferably all-butter (from one 17-ounce package), thawed

1 large egg, beaten with 1 tablespoon water, for egg wash

- Drizzle a 9 × 13-inch baking dish with the oil and use a brush to coat it evenly. Place the pizza dough on the prepared dish and stretch it toward the edges. If the dough is not moving to the edges, cover it with a kitchen towel and let it sit in a warm spot for 30 minutes, then try again.
- Preheat the oven to 400°F.
- Spread the tomato sauce evenly over the dough, then scatter the ham and cheese over the top. Sprinkle with the salt and oregano. Roll the puff pastry sheet into a 9 × 13-inch rectangle. Cover the dough with the puff pastry and brush it evenly with the egg wash.
- Bake for 40 to 45 minutes, until the pastry is puffed and golden brown. Remove from the oven and let cool for 10 minutes before cutting into squares. Serve immediately.

Biscotti Amaretti

AMARETTO COOKIES

Sardinians love these big soft amaretto cookies. When traveling through this beautiful island, almost every shop I visited had a giant cookie jar on the counter filled with their favorite cookie; I even saw them all over the airport in Cagliari, Sardinia's capital. Amaretti have a nice crunch on the outside and a soft center with a strong almond taste. Amaretti can be found all over Italy, but Sardinia's soft version is my favorite. If you don't have a piping bag, use a cookie scoop and make them as drop cookies. They taste delicious either way.

MAKES
30 cookies

3 cups (144 grams) almond flour

1½ cups (170 grams) confectioners' sugar

½ teaspoon kosher salt

Zest of 1 lemon

4 large egg whites, at room temperature

2 teaspoons almond extract

1 teaspoon amaretto liqueur (optional)

Slivered almonds, for garnish

- Preheat the oven to 325°F with a rack in the middle position. Line two baking sheets with parchment paper.
- In a large bowl, whisk together the flour, confectioners' sugar, salt, and lemon zest.
- In large bowl using a handheld mixer, beat the egg whites on high speed until soft peaks form, about 3 minutes. Add the almond extract and amaretto (if using) and beat to incorporate. Fold the egg whites into the flour mixture by hand until just combined.
- Fill a piping bag fitted with a star tip with about half the dough. Pipe circles of dough, about 1½ inches in diameter, directly onto one of the prepared baking sheets, spacing them about 1 inch apart. Place a slivered almond in the middle of each cookie.
- Bake on the middle rack for 10 minutes, until the cookies begin to harden and the bottoms are golden brown. Transfer to a wire rack to cool. Repeat with the remaining dough.

Canestrelli

EGG YOLK SHORTBREAD COOKIES

These lemon-scented, flower-shaped cutout cookies, found in Liguria, are made of a simple shortbread dough. What makes them different is the addition of hard-boiled egg yolks in the dough. Cornstarch contributes to their melt-in-your-mouth texture. They roll out quickly after an hour of chill time in the fridge. Cut out the centers with a small round cookie cutter and bake those off, too. A final dusting of confectioners' sugar truly gilds the lily.

MAKES
30 cookies

2 large eggs

2 cups (240 grams) all-purpose flour, plus more for dusting

1 cup (115 grams) confectioners' sugar, plus more for dusting

¼ cup (28 grams) cornstarch

2 teaspoons vanilla powder or pure vanilla extract

½ teaspoon kosher salt

Zest and juice of 1 lemon (2 teaspoons zest and 3 tablespoons juice)

2 sticks (226 grams) unsalted butter, cut into small pieces, at room temperature

◆ Place the eggs in a small saucepan, fill with enough cold water to cover, and bring to a boil. When the water boils, remove the pan from the heat and cover with a lid. Allow the eggs to sit for 10 minutes. With a slotted spoon, transfer the eggs to a colander and run under cold water until cool enough to handle. Peel the eggs and set the yolks aside; discard the whites or reserve for another use.

◆ In a food processor, pulse the hard-boiled egg yolks, flour, confectioners' sugar, cornstarch, vanilla, salt, and lemon zest to combine. With the motor running, add the lemon juice, then add the butter pieces one at a time and process until a dough forms.

◆ Transfer the dough to a sheet of plastic wrap and use the plastic to flatten the dough into a disk. Tightly wrap the dough in the plastic and refrigerate until firm, about 1 hour.

◆ Preheat the oven to 350°F. Line a baking sheet with parchment paper.

◆ On a lightly floured work surface, roll out the dough with a floured rolling pin to a ¼-inch thickness. Using a 2½-inch flower-shaped cookie cutter, stamp out as many cookies as you can. Transfer the cookies to the prepared baking sheet, placing them ½ inch apart. Using a ½-inch round cookie cutter, cut small holes out of the middle of each cookie. Gather the scraps, wrap in plastic, and chill for 20 minutes while the first batch of cookies bakes.

◆ Bake for 12 to 14 minutes, until the cookies are firm and the bottoms are golden. Cool completely on the baking sheet. Repeat with the remaining dough.

◆ Dust the cooled cookies with confectioners' sugar before serving.

Anicini

ANISE-FLAVORED BISCOTTI

Also called *finocchini*, these biscotti are very popular in Sardinia and Liguria. I was introduced to them by a friend who bakes them for Christmas. At the time, I was pregnant and found they instantly cured my morning sickness! While it might sound strange, there's something to this cookie's stomach-calming power. In Italy, aniseed is commonly used to soothe digestive upset. Drinking anise liquors like sambuca for *fine pasto* (end of the meal) is a tradition. My friend graciously shared her Italian grandmother's *anicini* recipe with me, so whenever a friend has morning sickness, I make a batch as a gift. They are much tastier than saltines. I love my biscotti with nuts, so I add almond slivers, but you can omit them.

MAKES
32 cookies

3 large eggs

1½ cups (300 grams) sugar

1½ sticks (169 grams) unsalted butter, at room temperature

1½ teaspoons pure vanilla extract or vanilla paste

1 tablespoon almond extract

4 teaspoons aniseed

3¾ cups (450 grams) all-purpose flour

2 teaspoons baking powder

¾ teaspoon kosher salt

1 cup slivered almonds (optional)

- Preheat the oven to 350°F degrees. Line a baking sheet with parchment paper.

- In the bowl of a stand mixer fitted with the paddle attachment, beat the eggs, sugar, butter, vanilla, and almond extract on medium-high speed until light and fluffy, 2 to 3 minutes.

- In a medium bowl, combine the aniseed, flour, baking powder, and salt. With the mixer on low speed, gradually add the flour mixture to the wet ingredients until just incorporated and a soft dough begins to form. Add the almonds (if using) and mix again just to combine.

- Dampen your hands with water to prevent sticking, then transfer the dough to a lightly floured work surface and form it into two equal-size balls. Place the dough balls on the prepared baking sheet. Pat them into two 3 × 11-inch logs. Make sure they are at least 3 inches apart.

- Bake for 25 to 30 minutes, until the logs have spread and are set but still soft to the touch. Cool on the baking sheet for 10 minutes; keep the oven on.

- Transfer the logs to a cutting board. Using a serrated knife, gently slice the logs crosswise into 1-inch-thick pieces. Arrange the pieces on the same baking sheet, cut-side down.

- Bake for 10 minutes, until the centers are cooked through and the biscotti are golden and crunchy. Let cool completely before serving or storing.

Torcetti

TWISTED BUTTER BISCUITS

Torcetti, which means "little twist" in Italian, are a simple biscuit from Northern Italy, known for their teardrop shape. I tried these light, buttery cookies in Valle d'Aosta with an afternoon coffee, and they were delicious: buttery and light, with just a hint of sweetness. They are also very easy to make. A buttered, yeasted dough is rolled out into cords, given a little twist, and shaped into an oval. Before baking, they are generously covered in raw sugar, which bakes into the dough.

MAKES
17 cookies

1 teaspoon active dry yeast

½ cup (113 grams) warm whole milk (110°F)

1¾ cups (145 grams) 00 flour, plus more if needed

½ cup (100 grams) granulated sugar

1 teaspoon vanilla powder or pure vanilla extract

¼ teaspoon kosher salt

1 stick (113 grams) cold unsalted butter, cut into small pieces

¼ cup (45 grams) turbinado sugar

- In a small bowl, whisk together the yeast and warm milk. (If using vanilla extract instead of powder, add it to the milk mixture as well.) Let stand for 5 minutes.

- In a medium bowl, whisk together the flour, granulated sugar, vanilla powder, and salt. Add the butter pieces, rubbing them into the flour mixture with your hands to coat them with flour and break them down into smaller pieces.

- Make a small well in the flour and pour in the milk mixture. Knead until the butter and flour are completely combined and a smooth ball of dough forms. (If the mixture is sticky, add 2 to 3 tablespoons more flour and knead until smooth.)

- Cover the dough with a kitchen towel and set in a warm spot to rise for 1 hour.

- Line two baking sheets with parchment paper. Pour the turbinado sugar into a shallow dish.

- Pinch off 1½ tablespoons of dough and roll it into a 10-inch rope. Give it a few twists and press the two ends together. Gently press the loop of dough into the turbinado sugar and then flip to coat the other side.

- Place 8 or 9 torcetti onto each prepared baking sheet, spacing them about ½ inch apart. Cover each sheet with a kitchen towel and set in a warm spot to proof for 1 hour. During the last 20 minutes of proofing, preheat the oven to 350°F.

- Place one sheet of torcetti on the middle rack and bake for 12 to 15 minutes. The tops will be pale golden, but the bottoms will be golden brown. Let the cookies cool on the baking sheet. Repeat to bake the remaining sheet of torcetti.

TORCETTI, PAGE 61

ANICINI, PAGE 60

PIZZICOTTI ABBRUZZESI, PAGE 72

MISTO BISCOTTI
€ 10,00
Kg

Brutti ma Buoni

HAZELNUT DROP COOKIES

Brutti ma buoni means "ugly but good" in Italian, and the name fits these cookies well. A mixture of egg whites and hazelnuts, these clunky cookies will not be the prettiest on the plate but are undoubtedly delicious. They can be found all over Northern Italy and are popular in Piemonte. These drop cookies will be sticky before they're baked and will have an irregular appearance, but once baked they will be light and crumbly and will melt in your mouth like a meringue. I love to add mini chocolate chips for extra sweetness.

MAKES
46 cookies

2 cups (300 grams) chopped hazelnuts

3 large egg whites

1 cup (200 grams) sugar

½ teaspoon kosher salt

1 cup (170 grams) mini chocolate chips (optional)

• Preheat the oven to 300°F. Place the hazelnuts on a baking sheet and toast in the oven for 3 to 4 minutes. Transfer to a small bowl to cool and line the baking sheet with parchment paper or a silicone baking mat.

• Place the egg whites in a medium bowl and beat with a handheld mixer on medium speed for 3 minutes. At the 3-minute mark, with the mixer running, add in ¼ cup (50 grams) of the sugar and the salt. Beat for 3 more minutes, until stiff and very glossy.

• With a rubber spatula, fold in the hazelnuts and remaining ¾ cup (150 grams) sugar. Transfer the mixture to a medium saucepan (set the bowl aside). Cook over low heat, folding the mixture and scraping the bottom and sides of the pan (some of the egg white mixture will stick), for 3 minutes, until the mixture begins to streak and turn pale golden. If you place a bit between your fingers, it should be tacky.

• Return the mixture to the bowl. Stir and fold the mixture to encourage it to cool. Once it is cool to the touch, about 5 minutes, fold in the chocolate chips (if using).

• Use two spoons to drop golf ball–size dollops of the mixture onto the prepared baking sheet, spacing them about ¼ inch apart.

• Bake for about 25 minutes, until the cookies are hard to the touch. Allow them to cool completely on the baking sheet before serving.

Baci di Alassio

DOUBLE-CHOCOLATE SANDWICH COOKIES

These chocolate sandwich cookies are from Alassio, a city in Liguria. These "kisses" are small chocolate cookies baked and then sandwiched with chocolate ganache. While they are similar in appearance to *baci di dama*, a Piemontese sandwich cookie, these are a rich dark chocolate cookie. They are unintentionally gluten-free, since hazelnut flour is used! Hazelnut flour can be difficult to find, but you can make your own (see Note) or simply use fine almond flour, which is my go-to. I also decided to upgrade the classic ganache filling with some toasted crushed hazelnuts, a splash of Frangelico to enhance the hazelnut aroma, and some flaky sea salt for the perfect finish. These are a perfect snack or an elegant addition to a holiday cookie platter.

MAKES
24 sandwich cookies

½ cup (75 grams) blanched hazelnuts

½ cup (113 grams) heavy cream

⅔ cup (2 ounces) chopped semisweet chocolate

⅔ cup (2 ounces) chopped bittersweet chocolate

1½ teaspoons kosher salt

1 teaspoon Frangelico liqueur (optional)

2½ cups (240 grams) fine hazelnut or almond flour

1 cup (200 grams) plus 4½ teaspoons sugar

⅔ cup (64 grams) unsweetened Dutch-process cocoa powder

3 large egg whites, at room temperature

1½ tablespoons honey

Cooking spray, for shaping the cookies (see Notes, page 66)

- Preheat the oven to 350°F. Line two baking sheets with parchment paper.

- Scatter the hazelnuts on one of the prepared pans and toast in the oven until fragrant, 5 minutes. Set aside to cool completely. Leave the oven on.

- In a small saucepan, heat the cream over medium-high heat until it just begins to boil. Turn off the heat and add the chocolate and ½ teaspoon of the salt, stirring to melt and incorporate the chocolate into the cream.

- In a food processor, pulse the toasted hazelnuts until broken down into small pieces but still coarse. Stir them into the ganache, along with the Frangelico (if using). Transfer the ganache to a small bowl, cover with plastic wrap, and refrigerate until it is the consistency of a spreadable paste, about 25 minutes.

- In a large bowl, whisk together the hazelnut flour, 1 cup (200 grams) of the sugar, the cocoa powder, and remaining 1 teaspoon salt to combine.

RECIPE CONTINUES

• In a large bowl using a handheld mixer, beat the egg whites on medium speed until soft peaks form, about 1 minute. Gradually beat in the remaining 4½ teaspoons sugar until the whites are stiff. Gradually add the whites to the flour mixture, beating to form a dough. Drizzle the honey into the partially mixed dough and beat until fully combined. At this point, you can use your hands to fold the ingredients together. The dough will be very tacky.

• Using a teaspoon or ½-inch cookie scoop, form the dough into small balls (you should have about 48 balls). Transfer to the prepared baking sheets, spacing them 1 inch apart. Spray your palms with a bit of cooking spray and press the dough balls gently into 1½- to 2-inch disks.

• Bake for 8 to 10 minutes, until crisp along the edges but still soft in the center. Let cool completely on the baking sheets.

• Using a small offset spatula or butter knife, spread a rounded teaspoon of the ganache onto 24 of the cookies, then sandwich with the remaining cookies. The cookies can be stored in an airtight container at room temperature for up to 10 days.

NOTES

To make your own hazelnut flour, toast 3 cups of hazelnuts in a 350°F oven for 5 minutes. Let cool completely, then pulse the nuts in a food processor until broken down into small pieces but still coarse. Scoop out ½ cup of the ground nuts and pulse until ground into a sandy flour; use this in place of the hazelnut flour called for in this recipe. The remaining flour can be stored in an airtight container in a cool, dry place for up to 30 days

Cooking spray is a wonderful tool when working with this dough. A little bit on your palms allows you to easily handle the sticky dough.

BISCOTTI AMARETTI, PAGE 57

BACI DI ALESSIO, PAGE 65

BRUTTI MA BUONI, PAGE 64

OCCHI DI BUE,
PAGE 70

STRAZZATE,
PAGE 71

MELIGHE,
OPPOSITE

Melighe

CORNMEAL WREATH COOKIES

The *meliga* is a simple cornmeal-and-flour-blended butter cookie from Piemonte. From the area of Cuneo, this variation was born in the mid 1800s, after the price of wheat increased and bakers started adding cornmeal to their desserts to keep their expenses down. The warm dough is piped out of a star-tipped bag to create a round wreath. It is said that Camillo Benso, the first prime minister of Italy, loved to dip them into a sweet wine like muscatel or dolcetto. They are also commonly served with zabaglione; however, they are perfect on their own.

MAKES
12 cookies

1½ sticks (170 grams) unsalted butter

1 cup (120 grams) all-purpose flour

1¼ cups (174 grams) fine cornmeal

1 teaspoon kosher salt

1 teaspoon vanilla powder or pure vanilla extract

2 large eggs

½ cup (100 grams) sugar

Zest of 1 lemon

Juice of ½ lemon

- In a small saucepan, melt the butter over medium heat. When the butter begins to foam, swirl the pan for 5 to 6 minutes, until the butter is browned. Set aside to cool for 5 minutes.

- In the bowl of a stand mixer fitted with the paddle attachment, combine the flour, cornmeal, salt, and vanilla.

- Crack the eggs into a medium bowl. Add the sugar and whisk by hand to just combine. Slowly pour the browned butter into the eggs, whisking as you pour. Add the lemon zest and lemon juice and whisk until slightly thickened, about 5 minutes.

- With the mixer on low speed, add the egg mixture to the bowl and mix until fully combined and a soft dough forms, 3 to 4 minutes.

- Preheat the oven to 300°F. Line a baking sheet with parchment paper.

- Transfer the dough to a piping bag fitted with a large star-shaped tip. Pipe 3-inch circles onto the prepared baking sheet, at least 1 inch apart. Bake for 20 minutes, until the bottoms have a golden brown rim. Remove from the oven and allow the cookies to cool to room temperature.

- Store in an airtight container at room temperature for up to 1 week.

Occhi di Bue

CHOCOLATE SANDWICH COOKIES

While the origins of this sandwich cookie are not confirmed, many believe it was created in Northern Italy, as it resembles the Austrian Linzer cookie. *Bue* means "ox" in Italian; the top cookie has a hole in the center, revealing the filling like a bull's-eye.

I enjoyed these cookies in Rome, where I found them in every pastry shop I entered. The variety of fillings was endless, but I always grabbed the one with a thick layer of chocolate-hazelnut spread. It's a perfect complement to the hazelnut flour I added to the dough. I also added a garnish of sea salt, which is not traditional but so delicious.

MAKES
24 sandwich cookies

2 sticks (226 grams) salted butter, at room temperature

1½ cups (180 grams) confectioners' sugar, plus more for dusting

1 large egg, at room temperature

1 teaspoon pure vanilla extract

1½ cups (170 grams) hazelnut flour or almond flour

2 cups (240 grams) all-purpose flour, plus more for dusting

½ teaspoon ground nutmeg

½ teaspoon ground cinnamon

1 cup (75 grams) Chocolate-Hazelnut Spread (see page 261)

Flaky sea salt

- In the bowl of a stand mixer fitted with the paddle attachment, beat the butter and confectioners' sugar on medium speed until light and fluffy, about 2 minutes. Beat in the egg and vanilla, scraping the sides of the bowl as needed, until the egg is just combined, about 1 minute. Add both flours and the spices and mix to combine completely. Transfer the dough to a large piece of plastic wrap, shape it into a disk, and wrap it in the plastic. Refrigerate for at least 1 hour.

- Preheat the oven to 350°F. Line two baking sheets with parchment paper.

- Remove the dough from the refrigerator and cut it in half. Return one half to the refrigerator. On a lightly floured work surface, roll the dough to ¼-inch thickness. Using a 2-inch round cookie cutter, cut out 16 rounds of dough. From 8 of the rounds, cut out a ¾-inch circle in the center (or use a fun shape, like a flower). Reroll the dough scraps and cut out another 16 rounds.

- Place the cookies and the cutouts on the prepared baking sheets and bake for about 10 minutes, until very lightly golden. Let the cookies cool completely on the baking sheets and repeat with the remaining dough.

- Fill a piping bag fitted with a medium star tip (Ateco #844) with the chocolate-hazelnut spread and pipe about 1 tablespoon onto each whole cookie. Lightly dust the tops of the cutout cookies with confectioners' sugar.

- Place the sugared cutout cookies on top of the whole cookies to create a sandwich. Sprinkle the chocolate-hazelnut spread peeking through the cutouts with flaky salt. Store in an airtight container at room temperature for up to 1 week.

Strazzate

DOUBLE-CHOCOLATE NUT COOKIES

These cookies are a chocolate lover's dream. From Basilicata, they double down on the chocolate, crackled with a hint of coffee and lots of toasted almonds. Traditionally, a bit of Strega, an Italian herbal liqueur known for its bright yellow color, is added, but it's tough to find in the States, and I found the cookies didn't need it to be delicious. If Strega is on your bar cart, add a tablespoon to the batter for a hint of something different—you'll taste mint, saffron, and juniper.

MAKES
40 cookies

1 cup (144 grams) almonds

1 cup (120 grams) all-purpose flour

½ cup (48 grams) almond flour

½ cup (42 grams) unsweetened Dutch-process cocoa powder

1 teaspoon kosher salt

½ teaspoon baking powder

½ teaspoon baking soda

10 tablespoons (141 grams) unsalted butter, at room temperature

1¼ cups (250 grams) sugar

1 large egg, at room temperature

2 teaspoons pure vanilla extract

1 teaspoon instant coffee granules

2 cups (340 grams/ 12 ounces) coarsely chopped semisweet chocolate or chocolate chips

- Preheat the oven to 350°F. Line three baking sheets with parchment paper.

- Scatter the almonds on a rimmed baking sheet and toast in the oven until fragrant and darkened slightly, about 10 minutes. Let cool for 15 minutes, then transfer to a cutting board and finely chop.

- In a medium bowl, whisk together both flours, the cocoa powder, salt, baking powder, and baking soda.

- In the bowl of a stand mixer fitted with the paddle attachment, beat the butter and sugar on medium speed until light and fluffy, 3 minutes. Add the egg, vanilla, and coffee granules, then beat until well combined, 2 to 3 minutes.

- Add the dry ingredients and beat on medium speed until almost fully incorporated. Turn off the mixer and stir in the toasted almonds and the chocolate. Mix on medium speed for an additional minute, until the nuts and chocolate are evenly incorporated into the dough and no dry flour remains.

- Portion the dough into 2-tablespoon balls (½ inch each) and arrange them 2 inches apart on the prepared baking sheets. Bake one sheet at a time for 10 to 12 minutes, until the cookies are set along the edges but still wet in the center. As they come out of the oven, firmly tap the baking sheet on the counter a few times to flatten the cookies (they will appear cracked on top). Let cool slightly on the baking sheets. Serve warm or let cool completely before serving or storing.

Pizzicotti Abruzzesi

FRUIT AND NUT FILLED PINCHED COOKIES

Most of my most cherished Christmas cookie recipes come from my mom. She always made several cookies for Christmas so we could give them to our teachers and friends. This recipe was given to her by a friend from Abruzzo. Typically, they are filled with chocolate or jam, but this version is extra special, as it has a fruit, chocolate, and nut filling. They're always in high demand, so she makes them every year. The fringed edges give them a delicate appearance, and they're dusted with confectioners' sugar for an extra hit of sweetness.

MAKES
24 cookies

DOUGH

2 cups (240 grams) all-purpose flour, plus more for dusting

2 sticks (226 grams) unsalted butter, at room temperature

4 ounces (113 grams) cream cheese, at room temperature

½ teaspoon kosher salt

1 egg, beaten with 1 tablespoon water, for egg wash

FILLING

½ cup mini semisweet chocolate chips

½ cup sweetened shredded coconut

½ cup walnuts, finely chopped

½ cup cherry jam

½ cup pitted dates, finely chopped

Confectioners' sugar, for dusting

- MAKE THE DOUGH: In a food processor, pulse the flour, butter, cream cheese, and salt until a soft dough forms, about 1 minute. Transfer the dough to a piece of plastic wrap and divide it in half. Shape each piece into a disk and wrap each one with plastic. Refrigerate for 1 hour.

- Position the oven racks in the upper and lower thirds of the oven. Preheat the oven to 375°F. Line two baking sheets with parchment paper.

- On a lightly floured work surface, roll one dough disk to ⅛-inch thickness. If the dough is too cold to roll easily, allow it to sit at room temperature for 5 minutes or so, then continue rolling.

- Using a knife or pastry cutter, cut out 3-inch squares. Gather and roll out the scraps and make more squares. Repeat with the second dough disk.

- MAKE THE FILLING: In a medium bowl, combine the chocolate chips, coconut, walnuts, jam, and dates.

◆ Spoon about 1 tablespoon of the filling into the center of each square. Fold 1 corner of the dough over the filling, then roll it over the filling so that the opposite corner overlaps the first corner and encloses the filling. Arrange on the prepared baking sheets, setting the cookies 1 inch apart. Brush the egg wash over the folded points to seal.

◆ Bake for 15 to 20 minutes, rotating the sheets from back to front and switching rack positions halfway through, until the cookies are set and golden.

◆ Let cool completely on the baking sheets, then dust with confectioners' sugar before serving.

CHAPTER 2

MERENDA

Afternoon Treats

Scarpaccia

SAVORY ZUCCHINI BREAD

On the Versilia coast in Tuscany, they are known for *scarpaccia*, a simple round zucchini bread. (The word roughly translates to "old shoe.") Unlike the zucchini cakes we typically have in the US, this bread is savory, not sweet. The zucchini is sliced instead of grated and Parmigiano Reggiano adds a nice cheesy note. Make sure to save some zucchini slices for a decorative topping.

MAKES
one 9-inch cake;
serves 8

½ cup (100 grams) extra-virgin olive oil, plus more for brushing and drizzling

2 cups (240 grams) all-purpose flour

1 cup (4 ounces) freshly grated Parmigiano Reggiano cheese

1 teaspoon kosher salt

½ teaspoon baking soda

½ teaspoon baking powder

3 large eggs, beaten

⅔ cup (150 grams) whole milk

1 cup (142 grams) toasted pine nuts

2 small zucchini (10 to 12 ounces total), sliced very thinly crosswise into rounds on a mandoline (about 3½ cups)

6 or 7 basil leaves, sliced into thin ribbons

- Preheat the oven to 375°F. Brush the bottom of a 9-inch springform pan with oil, line with parchment paper, and brush the parchment and sides of the pan with oil.

- In a large bowl, whisk together the flour, ½ cup of the Parmigiano, the salt, baking soda, and baking powder.

- Make a well in the middle of the flour mixture and pour in the eggs, milk, and the ½ cup (100 grams) oil. Whisk the wet ingredients to combine, then, using a rubber spatula, fold them into the dry ingredients. Fold in the pine nuts, followed by all but about 20 slices of the zucchini. Stir in the basil.

- Pour the batter into the prepared pan, spreading it into an even layer. Arrange the reserved zucchini on top in a circular pattern. Sprinkle the remaining ½ cup Parmigiano on top of the zucchini. Drizzle a few tablespoons of oil on top.

- Bake for 45 minutes, until the edges pull away from the sides of the pan and the cake is firm to the touch. The cheese and zucchini slices will be golden brown. Set on a wire rack to cool completely. Run an offset spatula around the edges of the zucchini bread to loosen before removing the sides of the pan, slicing, and serving.

Ciambella

VANILLA-CHOCOLATE-HAZELNUT SNACKING CAKE

In Italy, *ciambelle* are the quintessential snacking cake. Light and scented with vanilla, citrus zests, and fruit jams, they are easy to make and perfect with coffee, tea, or hot milk. I decided to glamorize mine by flavoring a little less than half of the batter with chocolate-hazelnut spread. Using a long skewer or butter knife, have fun swirling the two batters for a beautifully marbled effect. While this is perfect on its own for during-the-day eating, you can add the ganache to create a rich and beautiful after-dinner treat. Not a chocolate lover? Omit the chocolate and bake it up as a simple vanilla cake.

MAKES
1 large Bundt cake; serves 10

Unsalted butter or nonstick cooking spray, for greasing

2 cups (400 grams) sugar

1 teaspoon kosher salt

1 cup (237 milliliters) extra-virgin olive oil

¾ cup (170 grams) plain full-fat yogurt

½ cup (120 grams) mascarpone cheese

1 tablespoon pure vanilla extract

4 large eggs

1 cup (227 grams) whole milk

3 cups (360 grams) all-purpose flour

2½ teaspoons baking powder

1 tablespoon unsweetened dark cocoa powder

¼ cup (19 grams) Chocolate-Hazelnut Spread (see page 261)

Chocolate-Hazelnut Ganache (recipe follows; optional)

◆ Preheat the oven to 350°F. Coat a 12-cup Bundt or tube cake pan with butter or nonstick cooking spray.

◆ In a large bowl using a handheld mixer, beat the sugar, salt, oil, yogurt, mascarpone, and vanilla on medium speed for 1 to 2 minutes. (The batter will be very thick.) Reduce the speed to low and slowly beat in the eggs and the milk.

◆ In a medium bowl, whisk together the flour and baking powder (set the bowl aside). Carefully fold the flour mixture into the wet ingredients and mix with a spatula until just combined.

◆ Transfer about 2 cups of the batter to the empty flour bowl and add the cocoa powder and chocolate-hazelnut spread. Gently stir with a spatula until combined.

◆ Pour the vanilla batter into the prepared pan. Tap to even out the batter. Using a ladle or ice cream scoop, dollop the chocolate batter on top of the vanilla batter. With a butter knife or skewer, swirl the batters together, just enough to create a marble pattern, but do not mix them together.

RECIPE CONTINUES

• Bake for 1 hour 10 minutes, until the cake is golden brown and a toothpick inserted into the center comes out clean. Transfer to a wire rack to cool for 10 minutes. Remove from the pan and set the cake on the rack to cool completely. Pour the ganache over the cake, if desired; let set before serving.

CHOCOLATE-HAZELNUT GANACHE

MAKES ABOUT 2 CUPS

1 cup Chocolate-Hazelnut Spread (see page 261)
½ cup heavy cream
5 tablespoons unsalted butter, cubed
1 teaspoon kosher salt
2 tablespoons light corn syrup

Place the chocolate-hazelnut spread in a medium bowl.

In a small saucepan, heat the cream, butter, salt, and corn syrup over medium heat until just about to boil. Pour the hot cream mixture over the chocolate-hazelnut spread, allow to sit for a couple of minutes, then whisk until smooth. Set the ganache aside for 15 to 20 minutes to thicken before pouring it over the cooled cake.

Tazza di Torta

AFFOGATO MUG CAKE

Mug cakes became quite the rage in the States a few years back, and now they have made it across the Atlantic to Italy (I was excited to see *tazza di torta* popping up on menus during my last visit to Rome). I decided it would be fun to take my favorite Italian dessert, the affogato, which is simply a scoop of gelato served with a pour of hot espresso on top, and reinvent it as a mug cake. This cake is simple, with a rich middle from the chocolate-hazelnut spread. Then the espresso and gelato take you right to the edge—of the mug *and* your seat.

MAKES
2 mug cakes

6 tablespoons all-purpose flour

3 tablespoons sugar

¼ cup high-quality unsweetened Dutch-process cocoa powder

½ teaspoon baking powder

½ teaspoon espresso powder

¼ teaspoon kosher salt

6 tablespoons whole milk

6 tablespoons extra-virgin olive oil

6 tablespoons Chocolate-Hazelnut Spread (see page 261)

14 grams finely ground coffee beans, for espresso

2 scoops vanilla gelato

◆ Set a sifter over a medium bowl and spoon the flour, sugar, cocoa powder, and baking powder into it. Add the espresso powder and salt and whisk to combine. Add the milk, oil, and chocolate-hazelnut spread to the bowl and whisk to create a thick batter.

◆ Divide the batter between two mugs. Microwave both batter-filled mugs in 30-second increments for a total of 90 seconds, or until the cake has puffed and is cooked through.

◆ Use the ground coffee to brew two shots of espresso. When the espresso is ready, quickly place a scoop of gelato on top of each cake and pour a shot of hot espresso over each scoop. Serve immediately.

Migliaccio

LEMON RICOTTA AND SEMOLINA CAKE WITH BOOZY BLUEBERRIES

Migliaccio is a light, lemony cake traditionally made in Naples for Carnevale. While most Carnevale treats are fried and covered in sugar, this cake is a lemon-infused cheesecake enriched with semolina flour. To gild the lily, I added a lovely berry sauce with a splash of limoncello, the official liqueur of Naples, which complements the cake and dresses it up for company. This cake is surprisingly light with a hint of sweetness, and it's well suited for a midmorning snack alongside a frothy cappuccino.

MAKES
one 10-inch cake; serves 10 to 12

4 tablespoons (57 grams) cold unsalted butter, cut into 4 pieces, plus more for greasing

2 cups (454 grams) whole milk

2 cups (454 grams) heavy cream

2 cups (326 grams) very fine semolina flour

1 teaspoon kosher salt

2 cups (200 grams) sugar

5 large eggs

Zest of 4 lemons (about ¼ cup)

Juice of 1 lemon (about 3 tablespoons)

1 tablespoon vanilla paste or pure vanilla extract

1½ cups (375 grams) whole-milk ricotta

1 recipe Boozy Berries (recipe follows)

• Preheat the oven to 300°F. Butter a 10-inch springform pan.

• In a large Dutch oven, heat the milk and cream over medium heat until the mixture just begins to boil, about 10 minutes. Whisk in the semolina flour in a very slow stream. (Stop pouring and continue whisking if the semolina begins to clump.) When all the semolina has been incorporated into the liquid, stir with a wooden spoon for 2 minutes.

• Remove the pot from the heat and add the butter pieces. Add the salt and fold the butter into the mixture as it melts.

• Add the sugar and, using a handheld mixer on medium speed, beat the sugar into the batter until combined, about 1 minute. Add the eggs, one at a time, beating until the mixture is smooth and the eggs are fully incorporated, about 2 minutes. Add the lemon zest and juice and the vanilla and beat for 1 minute more. Add the ricotta and beat until the mixture is completely smooth and thick, 2 to 3 minutes.

• Spoon the batter into the prepared pan. (It will be very dense.) Smooth the top and bake for 1 hour 20 minutes, until the top is dry and slightly cracked in spots. (It will still have a slight jiggle.)

• Place the cake on a rack to cool completely in the pan. Serve at room temperature with the boozy berries spooned over the top.

BOOZY BERRIES

MAKE 1¾ CUPS

1 pint blueberries (about 2 cups)
Zest and juice of 2 lemons (about 2 tablespoons zest and 6 tablespoons juice)
¼ cup limoncello
2 tablespoons sugar

In a small saucepan, combine all the ingredients and bring to a simmer over medium heat. Cook until the fruit has broken down and a sauce has formed, about 5 minutes. The berry topping can be served warm or at room temperature. Store in an airtight container in the refrigerator for up to 1 week.

Crostata di Ricotta e Visciole

SOUR CHERRY CHEESE CROSTATA

Like many traditional Italian desserts, the origins of this crostata are historically significant. In the old Jewish quarters in Rome, at the Portico d'Ottavio, you will find this crostata prepared in the long-standing bakeries. In the eighteenth century, papal edicts prevented Jewish purveyors from trading dairy products, so bakers decided to hide the ricotta-based filling between pasta frolla dough and a jam of dark, sour visciole cherries. Visciole cherries are a wild Italian variety that are often preserved in syrup or made into jam so they can be enjoyed year-round. I was lucky enough to try this secret, heavily guarded, historic recipe at Boccione, a revered Jewish bakery, which was hard to find as they do not even have a sign on the door. While we do not have visciole cherries in the States, I have found sour cherry jam in Eastern European markets. Of course, you can also make your cherry jam. Either way, the results are sweet and tart. I opted for a lattice crust in my version because I felt that this beautiful filling should be celebrated after years in hiding.

MAKES
one 12-inch crostata; serves 8

PASTRY

3 cups (360 grams) 00 flour

1 cup (113 grams) confectioners' sugar

½ teaspoon kosher salt

¼ teaspoon baking powder

Zest of 1 lemon

2 sticks (226 grams) cold unsalted butter, cut into 1-inch cubes

1 large egg

2 large egg yolks

FILLING

2 cups whole-milk ricotta

⅔ cup confectioners' sugar

2 teaspoons almond extract

Unsalted butter, at room temperature, for greasing

1 cup sour cherry jam

1 large egg, beaten with 1 tablespoon water, for egg wash

RECIPE CONTINUES

◆ MAKE THE PASTRY: In a food processor, pulse the flour, confectioners' sugar, salt, baking powder, and lemon zest until combined. Add the butter, a few pieces at a time, pulsing after each addition. Then, continuing to pulse, slowly add the egg and egg yolks, one at a time, until just combined. Stop pulsing as soon as the dough begins to form.

◆ Transfer the dough to a lightly floured work surface. Knead until all the ingredients are combined and the dough is smooth. Flatten into a disk and cover with plastic wrap. Refrigerate for 1 hour.

◆ MAKE THE FILLING: While the dough is chilling, set a fine-mesh sieve over a medium bowl. Line the sieve with cheesecloth or a couple of layers of paper towels and spoon the ricotta into the lined sieve. Set aside to drain at room temperature for 1 hour.

◆ In a medium bowl, stir the drained ricotta, sugar, and almond extract together until fully combined. Set aside.

◆ TO ASSEMBLE: When ready to bake, preheat the oven to 350°F and lightly butter a 9½-inch fluted pie or quiche dish.

◆ Cut off about one-third of the chilled dough and return it to the fridge. On a lightly floured work surface, roll the remaining dough into a 12-inch circle. Place it in the prepared pan and press it to fit. Trim any excess dough.

◆ Spread the jam evenly over the dough, then pour the ricotta mixture over it, being careful not to mix it into the jam. Remove the reserved dough from the fridge and roll it into a 10-inch circle, then cut it into five 1-inch-wide strips. Weave the strips on top of the crostata to create a diamond-shaped lattice.

◆ Brush the lattice with egg wash and bake the crostata for 50 minutes, until the crust is lightly golden and the filling is set. Cool completely on a wire rack before slicing and serving.

Torta Russa di Verona

RUSSIAN CAKE FROM VERONA

This cake is the signature cake of Verona. When visiting this remarkable city, the birthplace of Romeo and Juliet, I was completely mesmerized by how quaint and beautiful it is—the perfect setting for the most famous love story of all time. Aside from the beautiful architecture and excellent shopping district, the food was delicious. I had one of the best lunches of my life at a small restaurant in the heart of downtown. At the end of this memorable meal, the server explained they only had one dessert to offer: *torta russa di Verona*. So we had to order it! Like Verona, it was charming and unique, a flaky puff pastry shell filled with a moist, nutty, buttery filling. The owner kindly shared the ingredients with me, so I could re-create it when I got home.

There are many stories about the cake's origins, but my favorite is about a local pastry chef who fell in love with a Russian girl. However, she was leaving aboard a ship to return home, so he ran to the dock carrying the cake he had made just for her. Unfortunately, she departed just as he arrived—like *Romeo and Juliet*, another tragic tale of unrealized true love. However sad the story, make this cake, and I assure you, it will be love at first bite.

MAKES
one 9-inch cake; serves 8 to 10

- 4 large eggs
- ½ cup (56 grams) confectioners' sugar, plus more for garnish
- 1 cup (200 grams) granulated sugar
- Zest of 1 lemon
- 2 sticks (226 grams) unsalted butter, at room temperature, plus more for greasing
- 3 tablespoons amaretto liqueur
- ½ cup (60 grams) ground amaretti cookies, homemade (see page 57) or store-bought
- 1 cup (116 grams) 00 flour, plus more for dusting
- 2 cups (192 grams) almond flour
- ½ teaspoon baking powder
- ½ teaspoon baking soda
- ½ teaspoon kosher salt
- 1 teaspoon vanilla powder or pure vanilla extract
- 1 (8-ounce) disk frozen puff pastry, preferably all-butter, thawed
- 2 teaspoons turbinado sugar

RECIPE CONTINUES

- Preheat the oven to 350°F.

- In a large bowl, combine 3 of the eggs, both sugars, and the zest. Using a handheld mixer, beat the ingredients on medium speed until pale in color and doubled in volume, about 5 minutes. With the mixer still running, add the butter and the amaretto and beat until fully combined, 2 to 3 minutes more.

- In a food processor, pulse the amaretti cookies into a coarse powder.

- In a large bowl, whisk together both flours, the crushed amaretti cookies, baking powder, baking soda, salt, and vanilla. In three additions, add the flour mixture to the wet ingredients, stirring after each addition, until fully combined.

- Place the puff pastry disk on a lightly floured work surface and roll until it is ¼ inch thick and 12 inches wide.

- Generously grease a 9-inch springform pan with butter or nonstick cooking spray. Line the pan with the puff pastry round, allowing the excess to hang over the edge. Pour the batter over the dough and spread evenly to the edges. Arrange the puff pastry overhang around the batter in a pleated pattern, similar to a galette. In a small bowl, lightly beat the remaining egg with 1 tablespoon water to create an egg wash, then brush it over the pastry. Sprinkle the pleated pastry edge with the turbinado sugar.

- Bake in the center of the oven for 55 minutes. The edges should be golden brown and the middle should be puffed and set.

- Cool on a wire rack for 10 minutes, then run a paring knife around the rim and release the sides of the pan (the center of the cake will have sunk slightly). Sprinkle with confectioners' sugar before cutting and serving.

Torta Tenerina

DECADENT CHOCOLATE CAKE

I'm a true chocoholic, so this cake hits all the right buttons for me. The first time I had it at Monteverdi, a beautiful villa in Tuscany, I had one of those "eyes rolling into the back of my head" moments, and realized I needed to create my own version. The cake's top puffs then cracks while baking, but the inside stays moist and soft. While the cake originated in Ferrara, it is now enjoyed all over Italy. The combination of hazelnut flour and high-quality chocolate brings so much flavor, and the boozy finish gives it the perfect kick. I love serving it with a small scoop of vanilla gelato. This cake is also gluten-free—and it tastes even better the day after it's baked, which makes it a perfect midday treat.

MAKES
one 9-inch cake;
Serves 8

1 tablespoon unsalted butter

1 tablespoon high-quality unsweetened Dutch-process cocoa powder

12 ounces high-quality semisweet chocolate, chopped

½ cup (100 grams) extra-virgin olive oil

½ cup (113 grams) whole milk

¼ cup Frangelico liqueur

6 large eggs, separated, at room temperature

½ cup (45 grams) hazelnut flour

1 teaspoon kosher salt

½ cup (100 grams) granulated sugar

2 tablespoons confectioners' sugar, for dusting

◆ Preheat the oven to 350°F. Butter the bottom and sides of a 9-inch springform pan. Sprinkle the cocoa powder over the bottom and sides of the pan and tap out any excess.

◆ Fill a small saucepan halfway with water and heat it over medium heat. Place the chocolate in a small bowl and set it over the saucepan to create a double boiler. When the chocolate has melted and is smooth and glossy, remove the bowl from the saucepan, add the oil, and whisk until fully combined. Add the milk and Frangelico, then whisk in the egg yolks, one at a time, until fully incorporated. Add the flour and whisk to incorporate.

◆ In the bowl of a stand mixer fitted with the whisk attachment, beat the egg whites and salt on medium speed until beginning to foam, about 1 minute. Add the granulated sugar and raise the speed to medium-high. Mix just until stiff peaks form, about 4 minutes.

◆ Fold the egg whites into the chocolate batter in three additions, then scrape the batter into the prepared pan. Bake for 30 to 35 minutes, until a toothpick inserted into the center of the cake comes out clean. Let cool completely in the pan. (The cake will fall and the crackly top will break up.) Sprinkle with confectioners' sugar right before serving.

Torta di Mele Invisibile

INVISIBLE APPLE CAKE

In Friuli-Venezia Giulia, apple cultivation occurs in the Carnian Alps area. Apple cider, traditional fare at weddings and baptisms, is sometimes referred to as the "wine of the poor." Every September, the Festa della Mela is held in Tolmezzo to celebrate the apple harvest. In this area of Italy, apples aren't just limited to sweets. For example, *cjalsons* are ravioli with an apple-and-nut filling, and *lasagne de fornel*, made for Christmas, replaces tomato and cheese with apples, seeds, and nuts. For this cake, you slice the apples very thin. They are folded into the batter and disappear into the cake as it cooks.

MAKES
one 9- to 10-inch cake; serves 8

1 stick (113 grams) unsalted butter, melted, plus room-temperature butter for greasing

5 medium sweet apples, such as Gala or Honeycrisp (1¼ pounds/ 575 grams)

Zest and juice of 1 lemon

4 large eggs

1 cup (200 grams) granulated sugar

3 tablespoons whole-milk ricotta

1 teaspoon kosher salt

1 teaspoon vanilla powder or pure vanilla extract

1½ cups (169 grams) cake flour

1 teaspoon baking powder

½ teaspoon baking soda

Confectioners' sugar, for garnish

• Preheat the oven to 350°F. Grease a 9- or 10-inch springform pan and line with parchment paper. Lightly grease the parchment.

• Peel and core the apples. Using a mandoline or very sharp knife, slice the apples very thin, dropping them into a medium bowl as you work. Pour the lemon juice over the apples and stir with a wooden spoon or spatula to coat.

• In a large bowl using a handheld mixer, beat the eggs and granulated sugar until pale yellow and thickened, about 2 minutes. Add the melted butter, ricotta, salt, lemon zest, and vanilla and beat for 2 to 3 minutes, until smooth and combined.

• Sift the cake flour, baking powder, and baking soda directly into the egg mixture and fold until just combined. Using a wooden spoon or spatula, mix the sliced apples into the batter, ensuring all the slices are coated.

• Pour the batter into the prepared pan and spread it evenly. Tap the pan on the counter a few times, then place it on a baking sheet. Bake for 1 hour. Let cool in the pan, then dust with confectioners' sugar before serving.

Torta Bertolina

GRAPE AND OLIVE OIL CAKE

This fruit-studded cake is from the city of Crema in Lombardia. It's known as a "nonna cake," as each grandmother has a version that she passes down to the next generation. The one common ingredient is the small sweet red grapes grown in the area, which are harvested in September and October. This cake can be served as a tart, crumb cake, or even as a tea bread. For my version, I created a moist, olive oil–laden cake and sprinkled the grapes throughout, using a larger pan so that it resembles a snacking cake. If you can find tiny Italian grapes, they will work perfectly. American grapes are typically larger and heavier, so if you use those, don't add the entire amount at once but instead reserve some to sprinkle halfway through the cooking process, so the cake will bake with grapes on both the bottom and top.

MAKES
one 9 × 13-inch cake; Serves 12

1½ cups (250 grams) extra-virgin olive oil, plus more for greasing

2 cups plus 2 tablespoons (268 grams) all-purpose flour, plus more for the pan

1½ cups (250 grams) granulated sugar

1 teaspoon kosher salt

1 teaspoon vanilla powder or pure vanilla extract

½ teaspoon baking soda

½ teaspoon baking powder

Zest and juice of 2 lemons

1½ cups (340 grams) plain full-fat yogurt

¼ cup (50 grams) limoncello

4 large eggs

2½ cups (400 grams) small or large purple grapes (see headnote)

Confectioners' sugar, for garnish

- Preheat the oven to 350°F. Line a 9 × 13-inch baking pan with parchment paper and lightly grease and flour the parchment.
- In a large bowl, combine 2 cups (240 grams) of the flour, the granulated sugar, salt, vanilla, baking soda, baking powder, and lemon zest.
- In a medium bowl, whisk together the yogurt, limoncello, oil, eggs, and lemon juice.
- Slowly whisk the wet ingredients into the dry ingredients, then whisk for 1 to 2 minutes more to remove any lumps, stopping once a smooth batter forms.
- Place the grapes in a medium bowl and mix with the remaining 2 tablespoons flour. If using small grapes, fold them all into the batter. If using larger grapes, fold 1½ cups of the grapes into the batter. Slice the remaining grapes in half and set aside.
- Pour the batter into the prepared pan and spread evenly. Bake for 25 minutes, until the cake has begun to set. If using larger grapes, remove the pan from the oven and sprinkle the reserved sliced grapes over top.
- Return the cake to the oven and bake for 20 to 25 minutes, until the cake is puffed and dry on top. Cool completely on a wire rack and sprinkle with confectioners' sugar just before serving.

Torta Caprese all'Arancia

ORANGE CAKE

A variation of the classic *torta caprese*, a delicious flourless cake from Capri, a magical island located in Amalfi, this moist, gluten-free cake is scented and flavored with citrus.

My family had the opportunity to visit the factory of Pasticceria Pansa, the most heavenly bakery located in the heart of Amalfi. There, the bakers taught us how to make candied orange slices, which they dip in chocolate and sell by the pound. I loved them so much, I decided to add candied orange slices to this recipe, sans the chocolate. The oranges need to be made ahead of the cake, as they need a day to firm up. Bonus: The cooking liquid from the candied orange slices transforms into a delicious glaze for the top of the cake.

MAKES
one 8-inch cake;
serves 6 to 8

Unsalted butter, for greasing

4 large eggs, separated

½ cup (100 grams) plus 1 tablespoon sugar

Zest and juice of 1 orange

1½ cups (144 grams) almond flour

1 teaspoon baking powder

½ teaspoon kosher salt

Candied Orange Slices and Orange Glaze (recipe follows)

- Preheat the oven to 350°F. Line an 8-inch round cake pan with parchment paper and lightly grease with butter.

- In the bowl of a stand mixer fitted with the paddle attachment, beat the egg yolks, ½ cup (100 grams) of the sugar, and the orange zest and juice on medium speed until fully combined, 2 to 3 minutes. Add the flour, baking powder, and salt and mix until incorporated. The batter will be very thick.

- In a medium bowl using a handheld mixer, combine the egg whites with the remaining 1 tablespoon sugar and beat on high speed until the egg whites have at least doubled in volume and soft peaks form, 3 to 4 minutes.

- Fold half the whipped egg whites into the batter, stirring somewhat thoroughly to initially loosen it. Then gently fold the remaining egg whites into the batter.

- Pour the batter into the prepared pan and bake for 25 to 30 minutes, until the top is golden brown.

- Remove from the oven and cool the cake in the pan on a wire rack for 10 minutes. Flip the cake out of the pan and onto a platter. Poke very small holes all over the top of the cake with a toothpick. Pour the warm orange glaze over the top and swirl to coat, allowing the glaze to soak into the cake (it's okay if a little drips down the sides). Once the glaze has been absorbed, decorate the cake with the candied orange slices.

RECIPE CONTINUES

CANDIED ORANGE SLICES AND ORANGE GLAZE

MAKES ¾ TO 1 CUP GLAZE AND 11 OR 12 SLICES CANDIED ORANGE

1 cup granulated sugar
1 medium orange
Olive oil or nonstick cooking spray, for greasing
¼ cup superfine sugar (see Note)
2 tablespoons unsalted butter
¼ cup heavy cream

Combine 2 cups water and the granulated sugar in a large, shallow pan with high sides and bring to a simmer over medium heat.

While the sugar mixture heats, thoroughly wash and dry the orange. Slice it into thin rounds, discarding the two outer slices.

Carefully add the orange slices to the simmering sugar syrup in a single layer. Shimmy the pan gently to help dissolve the sugar.

Reduce the heat to low and cook for 1 hour, until the pith is completely translucent. Check periodically; if the water evaporates too quickly, add another ½ cup water (you may have to do this more than once), so the sugar doesn't caramelize and darken.

While the oranges are cooking, line a baking sheet with parchment paper and place a wire rack on top. Grease the rack with olive oil or nonstick cooking spray.

Pour the superfine sugar into a bowl. When the oranges are cooked, place the slices, one at time, into the sugar, flipping to coat both sides and the edges. Set the coated oranges on the prepared rack and allow them to firm up overnight.

When all the orange slices are removed from the pan, add the butter and cream to the syrup and whisk to combine. Pour the glaze into a glass bowl or jar and reserve until ready to use (you should have a little less than 1 cup glaze). The glaze can be stored in an airtight container in the refrigerator for up to 1 week. Rewarm the glaze in a small saucepan for 2 to 3 minutes before pouring it onto the cake.

NOTE

If you don't have superfine sugar, place granulated sugar in a high-speed blender and blend on high for 10 seconds or so until the sugar granules become finer.

Sbrisolona

CRUMB CAKE

Sbrisolona is a popular dessert, originating in Mantua, near Lake Garda. In Mantuan dialect, *brisa* means "crumbs," and this dessert is known for the crumbling topping made of a mix of cornmeal, flour, and nuts. This simple dessert has been upgraded over the ages with fillings made of fruit, jam, cheese, and crème. I love chocolate so I added a rich homemade chocolate-hazelnut spread to the center. For the extra crunch, toasted hazelnuts are included, but almonds are also commonly used. Get creative with fillings and nuts.

MAKES
one 9-inch cake; serves 8 to 10

1 stick (113 grams) cold unsalted butter, plus more for greasing

1¾ cups (273 grams) fine cornmeal

1½ cups (174 grams) 00 flour

½ cup (48 grams) almond flour

½ cup (100 grams) granulated sugar

½ cup packed (106 grams) light brown sugar

1 teaspoon espresso powder

2 teaspoons baking powder

1 teaspoon kosher salt

2 large eggs

1 cup (75 grams) Chocolate-Hazelnut Spread, homemade (see page 261)

½ cup (71 grams) skinned hazelnuts, toasted and chopped

- Preheat the oven to 350°F. Butter a 9-inch springform pan and line the bottom with parchment paper cut to fit.

- In a food processor, pulse the cornmeal, both flours, both sugars, the espresso powder, baking powder, and salt. With the motor running, add the butter, 1 tablespoon at a time, until the mixture resembles small peas. (Alternatively, combine the ingredients in a large bowl and use your hands to incorporate the butter.) Add the eggs and pulse to form a soft, crumbly dough, scraping down the sides as necessary.

- Press half the dough, about 3 cups, into the bottom of the prepared pan, using a flat-bottomed cup to spread evenly as you press.

- Microwave the chocolate-hazelnut spread for 10 to 20 seconds, until it reaches a pourable consistency.

- Pour the warm spread onto the dough and spread it with an offset spatula, leaving a ½-inch border around the edge.

- Mix the hazelnuts into the remaining dough, then sprinkle them evenly over the chocolate. (Do not press them down.)

- Bake for 35 to 40 minutes, until golden brown on top and pulling away from the sides. Let cool completely on a wire rack before slicing and serving.

Torta delle Rose

ROSE WREATH CAKE

This brioche cake is similar to a cinnamon bun, with a sweet, leavened dough enriched and rolled with buttercream and topped with a delicate, lemon-scented glaze. The dough is cut and rolled to form roses, proofed, and baked in a round pan to create a beautiful bouquet. This cake is originally from the city of Mantua, in the region of Lombardia. It was baked for the wedding of Isabella d'Este and Duke Francesco Gonzaga in the early 1400s to represent the blossoming beauty of the young bride. Then the cake was given to new mothers as a snacking cake after childbirth. While the buttercream is traditional, feel free to substitute it with jams or chocolate-hazelnut spread.

SERVES
8

CAKE

¾ cup (171 grams) warm whole milk (110°F)

½ cup (100 grams) granulated sugar

1 (¼-ounce) packet active dry yeast (2¼ teaspoons)

1½ cups (174 grams) 00 flour, plus more for dusting

2 cups (240 grams) bread flour

2 large eggs, at room temperature, beaten

2 teaspoons vanilla powder or pure vanilla extract

Zest of 1 lemon

1 teaspoon kosher salt

10 tablespoons (141 grams) unsalted butter, at room temperature, plus more for the bowl

BUTTERCREAM FILLING

12 tablespoons unsalted butter, at room temperature

¾ cup granulated sugar

Zest of 3 lemons

LEMON GLAZE

1 cup confectioners' sugar, plus more for serving

Zest and juice of 2 lemons

- MAKE THE CAKE: In a small bowl, whisk together the milk, granulated sugar, and yeast. Let stand for 5 minutes.

- In the bowl of a stand mixer fitted with the dough hook, add both flours, the eggs, vanilla, lemon zest, and salt. With the mixer on medium-low speed, add the milk mixture and beat until just combined, 2 to 3 minutes.

- Turn the dough onto a lightly floured work surface and begin kneading it. Slowly drop pieces of the butter into the dough, kneading them in before adding a few more pieces until the butter dissolves into the dough and the dough is soft and supple. This should take about 15 minutes.

- Grease a large bowl with butter, place the dough inside, and cover it with a kitchen towel. Set aside in a warm spot to rise for 2 hours.

- MEANWHILE, MAKE THE BUTTERCREAM FILLING: In a medium bowl, stir the butter, granulated sugar, and lemon zest and mix with a spatula until fully combined.

- Generously butter a 10-inch fluted deep-dish quiche pan or springform pan.

RECIPE CONTINUES

• Place the dough on a lightly floured work surface and roll into a 16 × 20-inch rectangle. Spread the buttercream evenly over the dough.

• Cut the dough into eight 2-inch-wide strips. Roll each piece like a cinnamon roll and place them into the prepared pan, cut side down. Start with one roll in the middle of the pan and place the remaining seven rolls evenly around it with space in between.

• Cover the pan with a kitchen towel and allow the rolls to proof in a warm spot for 1 hour.

• Set a foil-lined baking sheet on the bottom rack of the oven. Place the second rack in the middle. Preheat the oven to 350°F.

• Bake the cake on the second rack for 35 to 40 minutes, until light brown. Tent with foil if it browns too quickly.

• MEANWHILE, MAKE THE GLAZE: In a medium bowl, combine the confectioners' sugar, lemon zest, and lemon juice and stir to create a brushable glaze (it shouldn't be a thick icing).

• While the cake is still hot, brush the lemon glaze over the top and let cool completely. Sift 2 to 3 tablespoons confectioners' sugar over the wreath just before serving.

Focaccia Genovese

GENOVA-STYLE FOCACCIA

While this famous bread dates back to ancient Rome, it has become the iconic bread of Genova. Focaccia's name is derived from the Latin, *panis focacius*, which means "hearth bread." In Italy, you will find it baked in wood-fired ovens, often alongside the bakeries' other specialties, like pizza and sandwich rolls.

The characteristics of focaccia are a fluffy, elevated height with a soft interior but a snap and crunch to the exterior from the generous amount of olive oil. For toppings, sea salt is the most common; however, there are so many variations, including onions, rosemary, potatoes, and even raisins and sugar. This recipe yields a straightforward focaccia, but feel free to add different toppings or spreads.

MAKES
one 13 × 18-inch focaccia; serves 10 to 12

DOUGH

1/2 cup (113 grams) warm whole milk (110°F)

2 teaspoons sugar

1 (1/4-ounce) packet active dry yeast (2 1/4 teaspoons)

6 1/4 cups (750 grams) bread flour, plus more for dusting

1 tablespoon kosher salt, plus 1 teaspoon for garnish

2 1/2 cups (600 grams) warm water (110°F)

1/4 cup (50 grams) plus 2 tablespoons extra-virgin olive oil

- In a small bowl, whisk together the milk, sugar, and yeast. Let stand for 5 minutes.
- In the bowl of a stand mixer fitted with the dough hook, combine the flour and 1 tablespoon of the salt. Mix on low speed to incorporate. (This can also be done in a large bowl with a wooden spoon.)
- With the mixer on low, add the water and mix until a shaggy dough forms, about 2 minutes.
- Add the milk mixture and mix to combine, about 1 minute. Do not overmix; the dough will be very wet.
- Transfer the dough to a lightly floured work surface. Using a bench scraper, carefully fold the dough into a messy ball so you can pick it up.

RECIPE CONTINUES

- Drizzle 2 tablespoons of the oil into a large bowl and swirl to coat the bottom and sides. Return the dough to the bowl, cover tightly with plastic wrap, and let rise in a warm spot until doubled in size, 1 to 2 hours.

- Pour the remaining ¼ cup oil onto a 13 × 18-inch baking sheet and place the dough on top. Press into the dough with all ten fingers, stretching it toward the edges of the pan. Once it begins to resist, loosely cover with plastic wrap and a kitchen towel, then let proof in a warm spot for 15 minutes.

- While the dough rises, place the racks in the middle and upper third positions in the oven. Preheat the oven to 425°F.

- Remove the towel and plastic wrap from the dough and begin pressing into the dough with your fingertips. The dough should easily move to the edges of the pan. Sprinkle with the remaining 1 teaspoon salt.

- Bake for 10 minutes on the middle rack, then rotate the pan and place in the top third of the oven. Bake for 10 to 15 minutes more. (The bottom should be golden brown, and the top will be puffed.) Serve warm or at room temperature.

FOCACCIA DELLA BEFANA, PAGE 110

FOCACCIA PUGLIESE, PAGE 112

Focaccia della Befana

SWEET FOCACCIA

In Piemonte, this sweet bread is prepared annually for the Epiphany (observed on January 6). Called the *focaccia della Befana* (named for La Befana, the old woman who, in Italian folklore, delivers presents to children on the eve of Epiphany), it's like traditional focaccia, but studded with raisins, candied fruit, and sometimes chocolate, and is served as a sweet treat for the holiday. Rum-soaked raisins are pressed into the soft dough and covered in sugar before it is baked. Instead of olive oil, butter is used for the gloss and shine.

MAKES
one 13 × 18-inch focaccia; serves 10 to 12

DOUGH

½ cup (113 grams) warm whole milk (110°F)

2 teaspoons sugar

1 (¼-ounce) packet active dry yeast (2¼ teaspoons)

6¼ cups (750 grams) bread flour, plus more for dusting

1 tablespoon kosher salt, plus 1 teaspoon for garnish

2½ cups (600 grams) warm water (110°F)

2 tablespoons extra-virgin olive oil

4 tablespoons (57 grams) unsalted butter, melted, plus more for greasing

TOPPING

2 cups raisins

1 cup dark rum

¼ cup sugar, for sprinkling

• In a small bowl, whisk together the milk, sugar, and yeast. Let stand for 5 minutes.

• In the bowl of a stand mixer fitted with the dough hook, combine the flour and 1 tablespoon of the salt. Mix on low speed to incorporate. (This can also be done in a large bowl with a wooden spoon.)

• With the mixer on low, add the water and mix until a shaggy dough forms, about 2 minutes. Add the milk mixture, then continue mixing on low to combine, about 1 minute. Do not overmix; the dough will be very wet.

• Transfer the dough to a lightly floured work surface. Using a bench scraper, carefully fold the dough into a messy ball so you can pick it up. Sprinkle a bit of flour on the dough, if needed, to release it from the surface.

• Drizzle the olive oil into a large bowl and swirl to coat the bottom and sides. Return the dough to the bowl, cover tightly with plastic wrap, and let rise in a warm spot until doubled in size, 1 to 2 hours.

• In a small bowl, combine the raisins and the rum. Set aside.

• Pour the melted butter onto a 13 × 18-inch baking sheet and place the dough on top. Press into the dough with all ten fingers, stretching it toward the edges of the pan. Once it begins to resist, loosely cover with plastic wrap and a kitchen towel, then let proof in a warm spot for 15 minutes.

• While the dough proofs, place racks in the middle and upper third positions in the oven. Preheat the oven to 425°F.

• Remove the towel and plastic wrap from the dough and begin pressing into the dough with your fingertips. The dough should easily move to the edges of the pan.

• Drain the raisins (discard the rum or reserve it for another use) and sprinkle them over the dough. Gently press the raisins into the dough and sprinkle the sugar over top.

• Bake for 10 minutes on the middle rack, then rotate the pan and place in the top third of the oven. Bake for 10 to 15 minutes more, until the bottom is golden brown and the top is puffed. Serve warm or at room temperature.

Focaccia Pugliese

TOMATO AND OLIVE FOCACCIA

In Puglia, focaccia is topped with tomatoes, olives, olive oil, and dried oregano. The dough is fortified with mashed potato and semolina flour, and the shape is round instead of square.

MAKES
one 10-inch round focaccia; serves 8

BREAD

½ pound russet potato (1 small or ½ large), peeled and cut into 1-inch pieces

1¼ cups (170 grams) warm whole milk (110°F)

1 (¼-ounce) packet active dry yeast (2¼ teaspoons)

1 teaspoon sugar

2½ cups (300 grams) bread flour, plus more for dusting

¾ cup (122 grams) semolina flour

1 teaspoon kosher salt

¼ cup (50 grams) plus 2 tablespoons extra-virgin olive oil

TOPPING

¼ cup extra-virgin olive oil

2 cups cherry tomatoes, halved

¾ cup dark olives, such as Kalamata, halved and pitted

2 teaspoons kosher salt

2 teaspoons dried oregano

Flaky sea salt, for sprinkling

- In a medium pot, combine the potato cubes with enough cold water to cover. Bring to a boil and cook until the potatoes are fork-tender, 10 to 12 minutes. Mash the cubes thoroughly with a fork or ricer (you should have 1 lightly packed cup/135 grams). Set aside to cool.

- While the potatoes are cooking, in a small bowl, whisk together the milk, yeast, and sugar. Let stand for 5 minutes.

- In a large bowl, combine both flours, the salt, and the cooled mashed potatoes. Mix with a wooden spoon to incorporate. Add the milk mixture and mix with your hands until a shaggy dough forms, about 2 minutes. (As the dough is forming, you can add a few tablespoons of water if needed to bring it together.)

- Transfer the dough to a lightly floured work surface and knead until it forms a smooth ball with a bit of bounce when you press it, about 5 minutes.

- Drizzle 2 tablespoons of the oil into a large bowl and swirl to coat the bottom and sides of the bowl. Place the dough into the prepared bowl, cover tightly with plastic wrap, and let rise in a warm spot until doubled in size, 1 to 2 hours.

◆ Pour the remaining ¼ cup oil into a 10-inch round baking pan and place the proofed dough on top. Press into the dough with all ten fingers to create dimples while stretching it to the edges of the pan. Loosely cover with plastic wrap and a kitchen towel and let proof in a warm spot for 15 minutes.

◆ While the dough proofs, place racks in the middle and upper third positions in the oven. Preheat the oven to 425°F.

◆ MAKE THE TOPPING: In a sauté pan, heat the oil over medium heat. Toss in the tomatoes, olives, salt, and oregano. Shimmy the pan, then cook for 5 minutes. Remove from the heat and let cool slightly.

◆ Spoon the topping, including the oil from the pan, evenly over the dough, carefully pressing the tomatoes and olives into the dimpled dough.

◆ Bake for 10 minutes on the middle rack, then rotate the pan and place it in the top third of the oven. Bake for 10 to 15 minutes more, until the tomatoes are lightly browned and tender and the bottom is golden brown. Serve warm or at room temperature.

Mozzarella in Carrozza

FRIED CHEESE SANDWICH

Mozzarella in carrozza is the closest thing Italians have to a classic American grilled cheese: molten mozzarella nestled between two slices of breadcrumb-coated, pan-fried bread. Serve with a side of marinara and you have the ultimate Italian rendition of a treat that satisfies a craving for a snack that's savory, gooey, saucy, and crunchy.

The origins of this sandwich have long been debated, as you can find them served across Italy, from Calabria to Naples to Venice, where they add prosciutto and anchovy. Everyone puts their own spin on it, but the foundation remains the same. The name itself also has an interesting backstory. *Carrozza* means "carriage" in Italian. Some believe the sandwich received its moniker because it resembles the carriage used to carry milk from the farms to the cities. Others insist that the long strands of cheese that pull from the bread as you eat it look much like the reins of horse-drawn carriages. Regardless of its origins, this sandwich has withstood the test of time, remaining a staple in Italian kitchens due to its simple ingredients and easy preparation, making it a very popular afternoon bite.

MAKES
4 sandwiches

3 large eggs

1 teaspoon kosher salt

1 teaspoon freshly ground black pepper

1 cup Cheesy Breadcrumbs (see page 267)

8 slices white bread, such as a Pullman loaf, crusts removed

16 ounces chilled fresh mozzarella cheese, shredded

¼ cup extra-virgin olive oil

- In a shallow bowl, whisk together the eggs, salt, and pepper. Place the breadcrumbs in another shallow bowl.

- Divide 8 ounces of the mozzarella among 4 of the bread slices. Top with the 4 remaining slices and press down on each sandwich.

- In a large skillet, heat the olive oil over medium heat until shimmering. Line a large plate with paper towels.

- Dredge each sandwich in the beaten eggs and then in the breadcrumbs, making sure to cover both sides and the edges of the sandwiches.

- Using your hands, carefully place the sandwiches, one at a time, into the hot oil and fry for 2 minutes, then flip and fry on the other side for 2 minutes more, until the breadcrumbs are golden and the cheese is melted. Transfer the grilled sandwiches to the paper-towel-lined dish to blot any excess oil. Serve immediately.

Piadina Romagnola

con Mortadella, Ricotta e Pistachio

FLATBREAD SANDWICH

Piadina is the sandwich bread of Bologna. The *piadinerie* that line the city's streets boast large sandwich boards listing the delicious combinations of fillings, savory and sweet, for this simple flatbread. One very classic combination is mortadella, the baloney of Bologna, and ricotta. I added pistachios here for crunch and a surprisingly delicious combination of flavors. The traditional piadina doesn't include potato, but I added some, taking a cue from the Pugliese and their delicious focaccia (see page 112), because I found it added a nice pliability when folding the bread in half after adding the fillings.

MAKES
8 piadina

PIADINA

8 ounces (225 grams) Yukon Gold potatoes, peeled and cut into 1-inch cubes

3¼ cups (390 grams) all-purpose flour, plus more for dusting

2 teaspoons kosher salt

2 teaspoons baking powder

3 tablespoons shortening or lard

¼ cup (57 grams) whole milk

Extra-virgin olive oil, for brushing

FILLINGS

1 cup whole-milk ricotta

1 cup shelled pistachios, toasted and chopped

Kosher salt (optional)

1 pound thinly sliced mortadella

- Place the potatoes in a medium pot, cover with cold water, and bring to a boil. Cook until the potatoes are very tender, about 12 minutes.

- Scoop out and reserve about ½ cup of the potato cooking liquid. Drain the potatoes and return them to the pot. Mash with a fork or a potato ricer. Add the reserved potato cooking liquid and whisk to combine and smooth out any remaining lumps. Set aside to cool, about 20 minutes.

- In the bowl of a stand mixer fitted with the dough hook, combine the flour, salt, and baking powder. Mix on medium speed for 1 minute. With the machine running, drop in small pieces of the shortening. Add the cooled mashed potatoes and milk. Raise the speed to medium-high and mix until the dough comes together into a loose ball, about 4 minutes. Transfer the dough to a lightly floured work surface and knead until a soft, pliable dough forms. Add more flour if needed.

RECIPE CONTINUES

- Roll the dough into a large log and cut into 8 equal pieces. (Use a kitchen scale if you have one; each piece should weigh about 4 ounces/115 grams.) Place on a baking sheet. Cover the dough with plastic wrap and allow it to sit for 25 to 30 minutes. (If you are in a rush, this step can be omitted.)

- Roll each piece of dough into a ball, then roll each ball into a flat circle, about 8 inches in diameter.

- Heat a flat-top griddle or large crepe pan over medium-high heat for 2 minutes. Brush with a few teaspoons of oil and reduce the heat to medium-low. Gently place one round of dough onto the griddle. Have a fork ready to prick the piadina if big bubbles begin to form. Cook for 2 minutes, until lightly browned. Brush the top with a bit of oil and flip. Cook for 1 minute more. Transfer to a wire rack to prevent the piadina from getting soggy. Repeat with the remaining dough.

- To make the sandwiches, spread a few tablespoons of ricotta over half of each piadina. Top each with 1 tablespoon crushed pistachios and a sprinkle of salt (if using). Add 4 or 5 slices of mortadella, fold the empty half over the filling, and serve.

Erbazzone

VEGETABLE PIE

This *torta salata* (savory pie) comes from Reggio Emilia and is a humble dish, prepared in bread ovens. It was traditionally a snack for farmers to eat as they tended the fields. Over time, a simple dough that was baked to make sandwiches for herbs and vegetable stems became enriched with greens like chard tossed with pork and onion. This recipe includes another delicious upgrade: mozzarella under the crust to provide a satisfying cheese pull. This sheet pan wonder is a filling snack or perfect for lunch with a lemony salad.

SERVES
8 to 10

FILLING

8 ounces pancetta, diced

4 tablespoons extra-virgin olive oil, plus more for brushing

2 medium onions, minced (about 3 cups)

3 garlic cloves, minced

2 teaspoons kosher salt

2 pounds Swiss chard, tough stems removed, leaves sliced into ribbons

1 pound frozen chopped spinach, thawed and squeezed of excess water

1 cup (2 ounces) freshly grated Parmigiano Reggiano cheese

3 cups shredded low-moisture mozzarella cheese

DOUGH

3 cups (348 grams) 00 flour, plus more for dusting

1 teaspoon kosher salt

2 teaspoons granulated garlic

◆ MAKE THE FILLING: In a large skillet, combine the pancetta and 3 tablespoons of the oil. Cook over medium heat for 7 to 10 minutes, until the pancetta is crisp and the fat has rendered. Using a slotted spoon, transfer the pancetta to a small bowl and set it aside. Pour all but a few teaspoons of the rendered fat into a small bowl and set aside (you'll use it for the dough). Do not wipe out the pan.

◆ MAKE THE DOUGH: In a food processor, combine the flour, salt, and granulated garlic. With the motor running, pour 3 tablespoons of the reserved rendered fat into the flour mixture. Slowly add ½ cup room-temperature water, mixing until the dough has come together but is still a bit tacky. Add up to ¼ cup more water if needed to bring the dough together.

◆ Transfer the dough to a lightly floured work surface and knead into a smooth ball. Knead for 8 to 10 minutes, until the dough is smooth and elastic. Place the dough in a bowl. Scrape any remaining rendered fat from the bowl you used for the pancetta fat onto the dough and cover with a kitchen towel. Allow the dough to rest for at least 30 minutes while you make the filling.

RECIPE CONTINUES

◆ Heat the skillet you used for the pancetta over medium heat. Add the remaining 1 tablespoon oil, the onions, garlic, and salt. Cook until the onions are translucent, about 5 minutes.

◆ Meanwhile, fill a large pot with 4 cups water and bring to a boil. Blanch the chard for 5 minutes. Drain and transfer to the skillet with the onions. Add the spinach and mix until the vegetables are fully combined. Remove from the heat and stir in the Parmigiano Reggiano and the cooked pancetta. Stir to combine.

◆ Preheat the oven to 350°F. Line a baking sheet with aluminum foil.

◆ Cut the dough into two equal pieces, about 12 ounces (340 grams) each. Roll one piece into a 9 × 13-inch rectangle (this is the bottom of the pie). Roll the other piece into an 8½ × 12½-inch rectangle (this will be your top piece).

◆ Place the bottom piece on the prepared baking sheet. Spoon the filling evenly over the dough, leaving a 1-inch border. Sprinkle the mozzarella over the filling in an even layer.

◆ Carefully place the top piece of dough over the filling, lining up the edges. Pinch and crimp the edges to seal. Brush the top and edges of the dough with oil. Prick the top of the dough with a fork to release steam as the pie bakes. Bake for 25 to 30 minutes, until the crust is firm but pale. Turn on the broiler and bake until brown, rotating the pan as needed, 3 to 4 minutes. Cool the pie on the baking sheet for a few minutes before serving.

Panadas

MINI MEAT PIES

Panadas are a savory meat-and-potato pie, that can be made large or small. The small ones, like these, are sold at the San Benedetto market in Cagliari, and are typically hand-shaped with a corded seam. Stewed lamb, potatoes, and sun-dried tomatoes are a typical filling, but the lamb can be replaced with pork or even artichokes for a vegetarian option. Once you get the method, the possibilities are endless.

MAKES
12 hand pies

8 ounces Yukon Gold potatoes (2 medium)

DOUGH

2½ cups (232 grams) 00 flour

½ cup (81 grams) semolina flour

1 teaspoon kosher salt

1 stick (113 grams) cold unsalted butter or shortening, cut into small pieces

½ cup (240 grams) plus 2 tablespoons ice water

FILLING

2 tablespoons extra-virgin olive oil, plus more for greasing

1 small yellow onion, minced

2 garlic cloves, thinly sliced

1 pound ground lamb

1 tablespoon kosher salt

1 tablespoon tomato paste

1 cup white wine

4 or 5 sun-dried tomatoes, minced and mashed into a paste

2 tablespoons chopped fresh flat-leaf parsley

1 large egg, beaten with 1 tablespoon water, for egg wash

• Place the potatoes in a pot with enough water to cover. Bring to a boil and cook until fork-tender, 25 to 30 minutes. Drain and set aside until cool enough to handle. Peel and cut into ¼-inch dice.

• While the potatoes cook, in a large bowl, combine both flours and the salt. Add the butter and work the flour mixture into the butter with your hands until the butter breaks down into very small pieces. Knead, adding a bit of water to incorporate the loose flour into the ball. When a shaggy ball forms, stop adding water. Transfer the dough to a lightly floured work surface and knead to form a smooth ball. Cover tightly with plastic wrap and refrigerate for at least 20 minutes.

• In a large skillet, heat the oil over medium heat. Add the onion and garlic and cook for 4 minutes, until the onion is translucent and the garlic is soft. Add the lamb and salt, breaking up the meat with a wooden spoon. Cook until no longer pink, about 2 minutes. Add the tomato paste and stir to combine.

• Raise the heat to medium-high and add the wine. Cook, stirring occasionally, until the wine reduces a bit, about 3 minutes. Add the sun-dried tomatoes and any juices from the cutting board and stir to combine. Remove the pan from the heat.

◆ Add the potatoes to the lamb mixture. Mix gently with a spatula, folding the potatoes into the meat until all the juices have been absorbed into the potatoes. Add the parsley, give it another stir, and set aside to cool.

◆ Preheat the oven to 350°F and grease a 12-cup muffin tin with oil.

◆ Roll out the dough to ⅛-inch thickness. Cut twelve 4½-inch rounds and twelve 3½-inch rounds tops. Fit the larger dough rounds into the prepared muffin cups, leaving an overhang at the top. Fill each cup with a rounded ¼ cup of the filling. Place the smaller dough rounds on top and press the bottom and top edges together to seal, crimping as you roll and pinch the seams.

◆ Brush the tops with the egg wash and bake for 45 minutes, until the tops are golden brown and the bottoms are cooked through. Run a butter knife around the edges and carefully tip them out of the pan. Serve hot or at room temperature.

Smacafam

SAUSAGE BREAD

This hearty casserole, with its unusual name, comes from Trentino. While recipes from Alto Adige have more of an Austrian influence, the cuisine of Trentino leans toward Veneto. Translated from the local dialect, "smacafam" means *scaccia fame*, or "hunger crusher." Caloric and dense, it is perfect for the cold winters of the Italian north. It's a combination of pork sausage mixed with a cheese batter that bakes up into a puffed bread, perfect for slicing and eating after coming in from the cold. Once baked, it will be soft, so resist the urge to slice in immediately—it is best served at room temperature, cut into thick squares.

SERVES
8 to 10

1 tablespoon unsalted butter, at room temperature, for greasing

2 tablespoons extra-virgin olive oil

1 small onion, diced (1 cup)

1 pound sweet Italian sausage, casings removed

Kosher salt and freshly ground black pepper

½ cup dry white wine

1½ cups (180 grams) all-purpose flour

½ teaspoon baking powder

½ teaspoon baking soda

2 cups (454 grams) whole milk

2 large eggs, beaten

8 ounces shredded low-moisture mozzarella cheese (about 2 cups)

- Preheat the oven to 350°F. Line a 9-inch square baking dish with parchment paper and grease generously with butter.

- In a large skillet, heat the oil over medium heat. Add the onion and cook, stirring occasionally, until translucent, about 5 minutes. Add the sausage and season with salt and pepper. Cook, stirring and breaking it up into small pieces with a wooden spoon, until the sausage is no longer pink, 2 to 3 minutes. Deglaze the pan with the wine and cook until the wine has almost completely evaporated, about 5 minutes. Remove from the heat and allow the mixture to cool.

- In a large bowl, whisk together the flour, baking powder, baking soda, milk, eggs, and 1 teaspoon each of salt and pepper until a thin batter forms. (The batter will be thinner than a pancake batter.) Pour the batter into the prepared baking dish. Sprinkle the sausage mixture evenly over the top. Sprinkle the mozzarella evenly over the sausage.

- Bake for 45 minutes to 1 hour, until the middle is puffed and the edges are golden brown. Cool the bread on a wire rack for 30 minutes. Cut into squares and serve warm or at room temperature.

Panna Cotta Piemontese

CHOCOLATE-HAZELNUT PANNA COTTA

Panna cotta, a classic Italian dessert, starts as a thin mixture that comes together with a few simple steps followed by an overnight stay in the refrigerator, where a rich custard develops. Traditionally, it's vanilla-scented, but it's always okay to break the rules with chocolate, especially when chocolate-hazelnut spread, a decadent and quite famous treat from Piemonte, is involved. Serve this panna cotta with whipped cream, berries, and nuts for a treat that is the height of decadence.

SERVES
6

Olive oil, for greasing

1 (¼-ounce) envelope unflavored powdered gelatin

1½ cups heavy cream

1 cup half-and-half or whole milk

2 ounces high-quality dark chocolate, coarsely chopped

1 cup Chocolate-Hazelnut Spread (see page 261)

½ teaspoon kosher salt

1 cup Noci Croccante (see page 260)

FOR SERVING

Whipped cream, orange zest, and fresh raspberries

- Lightly oil six 4-ounce ramekins and place them on a baking sheet.
- In a medium bowl, sprinkle the gelatin over ¼ cup cold water and whisk to combine. Let stand for at least 5 minutes to bloom the gelatin.
- In a medium saucepan, bring the half-and-half to a boil over medium heat. Turn off the heat and pour half the hot cream over the gelatin, whisking to combine. Add the chocolate, chocolate-hazelnut spread, and salt to the saucepan with the remaining half-and-half. Mix until both the spread and the chocolate have completely melted and the mixture is combined.
- Add the gelatin mixture to the saucepan and whisk again until smooth. Transfer the mixture to a large heatproof glass measuring cup with a spout and divide it evenly among the ramekins. Refrigerate, uncovered, for at least 6 hours or up to overnight before serving.
- Run a butter knife around the edge of each panna cotta and flip them onto individual serving dishes (see Note). You can also serve them directly from the ramekins. Sprinkle with noci croccante and top with whipped cream and orange zest. Serve with fresh raspberries alongside.

NOTE

If the panna cotta doesn't release, run the butter knife around the edge, then dip the bottom of the ramekin into a bowl of hot water for 5 seconds and flip it over to release.

Biancomangiare

WHITE PUDDING

This sweet almond pudding is found throughout Europe, though its origins are French. There it is known as blancmange, from the Anglo-French *blanc manger*, meaning "white food." It is prepared in various iterations throughout Italy; I saw it made with almond milk in Sardinia and Sicily, while up north in Valle d'Aosta, it is made with whole milk or cream. Though traditionally this is an all-white dessert, I added a bit of chocolate as a fun surprise. Made with almond milk and without cream or chocolate, it is a great dairy-free and gluten-free snack. The pudding comes together in minutes thanks to the cornstarch, so I make them the night before or early in the morning, and they are ready when the kids get off the bus. Have fun with the toppings and to make it a bit fancy, use a pretty ramekin or mold like they do in Europe.

MAKES
4 puddings

4 cups whole milk or unsweetened almond milk

½ cup cornstarch, sifted

¼ teaspoon kosher salt

¾ cup sugar

½ teaspoon almond extract

½ cup dark chocolate chips (optional)

¼ cup heavy cream (optional)

GARNISHES

2 to 3 teaspoons ground cinnamon

2 to 3 teaspoons unsweetened Dutch-process cocoa powder

½ cup chopped toasted pistachios

- In a large saucepan, heat the milk over medium heat. When you begin to see bubbles along the sides of the pan, about 2 minutes, add the cornstarch and whisk to combine. Raise the heat to medium-high and add the salt and sugar. Whisk until fully combined and the mixture has begun to thicken and boil, 5 minutes. Remove from the heat and whisk the pudding for another minute to release some of the heat.

- In a small bowl, combine the chocolate chips and cream (if using). Microwave for 30 seconds, stir, then microwave for another 30 seconds, until the chocolate has melted. Stir until the chocolate sauce is fully combined and smooth.

- Spoon ½ cup of the pudding into the bottom of each of four clear heatproof glasses or ramekins. Spoon 2 teaspoons of the chocolate sauce into each cup. Divide the remaining pudding among the cups. Cover with plastic wrap and refrigerate for 3 to 4 hours before serving. Garnish with the cinnamon, cocoa powder, pistachios, or all three!

Budino di Riso

RICE PUDDING CUPS

As a child, I was fortunate enough to spend summers in Florence. My father, a university professor, taught in a summer abroad program for students, so my mother, sister, and I would tag along and enjoy the Tuscan sun.

My favorite midmorning ritual during those summers was thick, hot chocolate and a *budino di riso*, a baked rice pudding, from Caffè Gilli, packaged in a delicate pie crust and dusted with confectioners' sugar. My parents would order coffee in this boisterous bar while I patiently waited for this doily-wrapped confection to land in my hand. I would stand in front of the Duomo devouring it, already anticipating when I could have another. I loved them so much that years later, when my sister studied abroad in Italy, she smuggled one back in her suitcase for me.

As an adult, I began, through many trials, to match the exact flavor and texture of my favorite Florentine dessert. I also did some research and found that this little pudding began, not surprisingly, in the homes of Tuscan nonnas who would make a large pot of rice pudding and then bake them (no crust) into individual puddings to give to their hungry grandchildren after school for merenda. Later, pastry shops added the crust to make them a bit fancier and easier to eat.

MAKES
12 puddings

PASTA FROLLA

2 cups (240 grams) all-purpose flour

⅓ cup (66 grams) granulated sugar

1 teaspoon baking powder

1 teaspoon kosher salt

1 stick (113 grams) cold unsalted butter, cut into tablespoon-size pieces

2 large eggs

2 teaspoons vanilla paste or pure vanilla extract

Zest of 1 large lemon

RICE PUDDING FILLING

3 tablespoons unsalted butter, plus more for greasing

½ cup Arborio rice

¼ cup vin santo or sweet Marsala wine

2 cups whole milk, plus up to ¼ cup, as needed

½ cup granulated sugar

1 tablespoon vanilla paste or pure vanilla extract

2 large eggs, beaten

Zest of 1 lemon

½ cup confectioners' sugar, for dusting

RECIPE CONTINUES

◆ MAKE THE PASTA FROLLA: In a food processor, pulse the flour, granulated sugar, baking powder, and salt four or five times to combine. With the motor running, slowly add the butter, 1 tablespoon at a time, until fully incorporated, 2 to 3 minutes. Add the eggs one at a time. Add the vanilla and lemon zest and pulse again. Continue to pulse until a dough forms.

◆ Transfer the dough to a lightly floured work surface. Form into a large disk and cover with plastic wrap. Refrigerate for 30 minutes.

◆ MEANWHILE, MAKE THE FILLING: In a large heavy-bottomed pot, melt the butter over medium heat. Add the rice and stir to combine with the melted butter. Add the vin santo and stir until it has almost evaporated, about 2 minutes. Slowly add the milk and stir to combine. Stir in the granulated sugar and vanilla. Bring to a boil, then quickly reduce the heat to maintain a simmer. Cook, stirring occasionally, for 25 to 30 minutes, until the mixture has reduced and the rice is plump, thickened, and tender. The mixture should be thick but not dry. If it seems too dry, add another ¼ cup milk.

◆ Slowly add the eggs, stirring vigorously to prevent them from scrambling. Add the lemon zest, stir to combine, and remove from the heat. Set aside to cool.

◆ Preheat the oven to 350°F. Heavily grease a 12-cup muffin tin.

◆ Roll out the pasta frolla to a ¼-inch thickness and cut into twelve 3½-inch rounds. Press each round into one of the prepared muffin cups. There should be a small overhang at the top. Line each with a square of parchment paper and add some pie weights. Bake for 10 minutes, until just set. Remove the parchment and pie weights and allow to cool.

◆ Fill each of the parbaked crusts to the top with the cooled rice pudding. Bake for 20 minutes, until the tops are lightly golden and the rice pudding has puffed. Let cool completely.

◆ To serve, sift the confectioners' sugar over the top. Leftover budino di riso can be stored in an airtight container in the refrigerator for up to 1 week.

Ciocccolato da Taglio

SLICEABLE CHOCOLATE SNACKING BAR

When I was a child, my grandmother would send us care packages from Italy. They usually consisted of good espresso beans, a few kinds of hard cheese, some hard candy, and a large bar of chocolate. This bar wasn't a candy bar—it was a heavy, loaf-size chocolate studded with hazelnuts. The chocolate was just soft enough to cut into slices and eat by the piece or spread onto a slice of bread. I loved this bar, as it came in dark chocolate, white chocolate, or sometimes a combination of the two. I have never been able to find anything like it here in the States, so using a silicone loaf pan that the chocolate will not stick to, I started making it at home. I love adding a bit of texture to one of the layers, so French *feuilletine* or crispy rice cereal is mixed in. While it is sold commercially all over Italy, this snacking bar is prepared by chocolatiers on All Souls' Day (November 2) in Naples.

MAKES
one 9-inch chocolate bar; serves 8 to 10

1¼ cups chopped bittersweet chocolate

1¼ cups chopped semisweet chocolate

1 cup Chocolate-Hazelnut Spread (see page 261)

2 cups chopped white chocolate

1 cup hazelnuts, toasted

½ cup feuilletine flakes or crispy rice cereal, such as Rice Krispies

- Fill a medium saucepan halfway with water and bring to a simmer over medium heat.

- Find three heatproof medium bowls that will fit over the top of the saucepan to create a double boiler for melting the chocolate: Place the bittersweet chocolate in one bowl, the semisweet chocolate and ¾ cup of the chocolate-hazelnut spread in the second bowl, and the white chocolate and remaining ¼ cup chocolate-hazelnut spread in the third bowl.

- Set the bowl with the bittersweet chocolate over the saucepan of simmering water. Stir gently until it has completely melted. Scoop out ¼ cup of the melted bittersweet chocolate and set aside. Pour the remaining melted chocolate into a 9 × 3½ × 2½-inch silicone loaf pan. Using a small offset spatula or silicone pastry brush, spread the chocolate up all sides of the pan and evenly over the bottom to create a very thin layer (this will be the outer shell). Refrigerate to set the chocolate.

RECIPE CONTINUES

◆ Set the bowl of semisweet chocolate and chocolate-hazelnut spread over the simmering water. When it has melted, add the hazelnuts and feuilletine and stir to combine. Take the loaf pan out of the fridge. (The bittersweet chocolate will have already begun to set.) Pour the melted chocolate-nut mixture into the loaf pan and spread it evenly over the bittersweet chocolate base. Return the pan to the refrigerator.

◆ Place the bowl of white chocolate and chocolate-hazelnut spread over the simmering water. When it has melted, stir to combine. Remove the loaf pan from the fridge and pour the melted white chocolate mixture over the chocolate-nut layer and spread it evenly. Return the pan to the refrigerator.

◆ Rewarm the reserved ¼ cup melted bittersweet chocolate over the simmering water. Remove the loaf pan from the fridge and pour the melted bittersweet chocolate over the white chocolate layer; it should reach the top of the pan. Spread it evenly (this will be the bottom layer of the snacking bar). Return the loaf pan to the fridge once more and chill for at least 1 hour.

◆ When ready to serve, flip the pan onto a serving platter and carefully remove the pan from the snacking bar. Let the bar sit for 30 minutes before slicing and serving.

Cioccolata Calda

HOT CHOCOLATE

This hot beverage is a Florentine tradition. Served at the bars, it's velvety and so thick, it feels more like a pudding than a beverage. When visiting Florence, my father would bring us to Caffè Rivoire, right in front of Palazzo Vecchio. The recipe is a highly coveted secret, but, with a bit of tinkering, I believe I have created a respectable replica. If they can do it with Michelangelo's David, I can do it too, right?

SERVES
4

3 cups whole milk

¼ cup heavy cream

1 tablespoon cornstarch

4 ounces bittersweet chocolate (70% cacao), finely chopped

¼ to ½ cup sugar, to taste

◆ In a large saucepan, combine the milk and cream and heat over medium heat until the mixture begins to bubble, about 2 minutes. Whisk in the cornstarch and cook for 2 to 3 minutes more. Add the chocolate and whisk to combine. Pour in ¼ cup of the sugar, whisking to combine. Cook, whisking continuously, for 4 to 5 minutes more, until the mixture is thick and coats the back of a spoon. Remove from the heat. Taste for sweetness and whisk in more sugar, if desired. Pour into cups and enjoy immediately, with a spoon.

Limoncello Sorbetto

LIMONCELLO SORBET

This limoncello sorbet is summer in a lemon cup, a refreshing treat with the perfect balance of sweet and tart. It's even a little creamy, thanks to the egg whites. In Italy, this sorbet is often served at weddings as an after-dinner digestive, but it's also a sought-after snack on a hot summer day. Whenever I make this, I am transported to one of my favorite places, the Amalfi coast. Amalfi lemons are gorgeous and huge; they are used in many of the area's savory and sweet treats, but perhaps most famously they are the base of the lemony liqueur limoncello.

If you would like a quicker result, feel free to make the sorbetto in an ice cream maker, but if you plan ahead, it can be frozen right in the lemon cups for a fun and pretty presentation. The recipe makes more sorbet than is needed for the eight lemon cups so store the rest in a freezer-safe container for up to a week.

MAKES
5 cups

5 large lemons

1 cup plus
1 teaspoon sugar

1 shot (1½ ounces)
limoncello

1 egg white

8 mint leaves,
for garnish

• Cut 4 of the lemons in half lengthwise. Slice a bit of lemon rind off the rounded side so that each half can stand cut-side up without tipping (reserve the bits you slice off as well).

• Using a paring knife and a spoon (a grapefruit spoon works great), remove all the pulp from the inside of the lemon halves without cutting through the rind. Place the lemon cups on a baking sheet and place in the freezer until ready to fill.

• Transfer the lemon pulp, seeds, and interior flesh to a medium saucepan. Add the cut rind pieces, too.

• Zest the remaining lemon into the saucepan. Cut the lemon in quarters, then squeeze the juice into the pot. Drop the squeezed lemon wedges into the pan. Add 4 cups water, 1 cup of the sugar, and the limoncello and stir to combine. Bring to a boil, then cook, stirring to dissolve the sugar, for 2 minutes. Remove from the heat and set aside to cool completely, about 1 hour.

• In a medium bowl using a handheld mixer, beat the egg white with the remaining 1 teaspoon sugar on medium speed until stiff peaks form, 4 to 5 minutes.

• Strain the cooled lemon mixture into a large bowl and discard the solids. Slowly fold the egg white into the lemon mixture. Whisk vigorously until fully combined. (It will separate, and that is okay.) Fill the frozen lemon cups to the brim with the lemon mixture. You will have some

left over in the bowl; place the bowl and the filled lemon cups in the freezer. After 1 hour, remove the bowl from the freezer and whisk the sorbetto. Return it to the freezer for at least 3 to 4 hours, until set.

◆ Spoon generous amounts of sorbetto from the bowl onto the frozen lemon cups to create a dome on top. Return the lemon cups to the freezer for at least 1 hour before serving.

Espresso Martini Granita

ESPRESSO-FLAVORED SHAVED ICE

Granita is a frozen, icy dessert hailing from Sicily. Fresh fruits like strawberry or lemon are pureed and frozen with water to create an icy, flaked treat served in a fancy glass to cool down on a hot summer day. But Italians love their coffee, so there is also a fun variation that, along with a cool-down, gives you a nice shot of caffeine. This recipe is a slightly boozy upgrade that adds some coffee liqueur and vodka turns the granita into a frozen martini.

SERVES
4

2 cups (16 ounces) hot espresso or regular brewed coffee

¼ cup sugar

2 tablespoons coffee liqueur

¼ cup vodka

Whipped cream, for serving

Espresso beans, for garnish (optional)

- Immediately after brewing the espresso, pour it into a 9 × 13-inch baking dish, then add the sugar and stir to dissolve. Add the coffee liqueur, vodka, and 2 cups water. Stir to combine and place in the freezer for 1 hour.

- Remove the baking dish from the freezer and mix with a fork to disrupt the forming ice crystals. Return the dish to the freezer for 30 minutes.

- Remove the baking dish from the freezer again and, using a fork, scrape the surface to create shards of ice. Repeat three or four more times at 30-minute intervals until the granita has a rough, hardened consistency.

- Dollop a few teaspoons of whipped cream into four martini glasses. Spoon the granita on top, then add more whipped cream over the granita. Garnish with a few espresso beans, if desired, and serve immediately. Leftover granita can be stored in the freezer, covered, for up to 1 week. Flake again with a fork before serving.

Frittelle di Mele

APPLE FRITTERS

Apples are one of the signature ingredients of Trentino–Alto Adige in Northern Italy. This area has one of the world's largest producers of high-quality apple cultivation. Like many Italian food products, they are regulated with strict quality control. Apples figure into many of the region's desserts and savory dishes. One such dish is *frittelle di mele*, apple fritters.

What I love about Italian apple fritters is that instead of chopping the apples into pieces and frying up balls of dough, as is commonly done here in the States, the apples are peeled, cored, and thinly sliced before being battered. The result is a delicate and thin apple pancake that resembles a doughnut (due to the cored apple center). While these fritters taste delicious with a dusting of confectioners' sugar, I have also enjoyed them with a drizzle of honey and a thin slice of prosciutto. Paired with a crisp glass of white wine and a bit of cheese, this makes for the most special aperitivo!

MAKES
20 fritters; serves 4 or 5

1½ cups (340 grams) whole milk

Zest and juice of 1 lemon

1½ cups (180 grams) all-purpose flour

3 tablespoons sugar

2 teaspoons baking powder

1 teaspoon kosher salt

1 tablespoon extra-virgin olive oil

5 large sweet apples, such as Honeycrisp or Gala

2 cups neutral oil, such as canola or grapeseed, for frying

20 prosciutto slices

Honey, for drizzling

- Pour the milk into a spouted measuring cup and stir in the lemon juice. Set aside.

- In a large bowl, combine the flour, lemon zest, sugar, baking powder, salt, and olive oil. Pour in the milk mixture and whisk to form a thick batter.

- Let the batter stand for 10 minutes.

- Peel and core the apples. Cut each apple into thin slices (about ⅛ inch thick; use a mandoline to keep the slices consistent and very thin).

- In a cast-iron skillet, heat 1 cup of the neutral oil over medium heat until it begins to shimmer. Line a baking sheet with parchment paper and set a wire rack on top.

- Dredge the apple slices in the batter and carefully place 3 or 4 into the hot oil. Fry until the batter begins to crisp and brown, about 2 minutes. Flip and cook for 2 minutes more, until both sides are golden brown and the batter has puffed. Prick an apple slice with a fork. If the apple is still a bit hard, flip again and cook until the apple is soft. Transfer the cooked fritters to the rack. Immediately lay a piece of prosciutto over each apple fritter. Repeat to cook the remaining apples, adding more oil as needed between batches.

- Drizzle the fritters with honey and serve immediately.

Cassatelle

CRESCENT HAND PIES

These sugar-dusted, half-moon pastries originated in the Sicilian province of Trapani but are enjoyed all over the island. While it is a tradition to eat them for Carnevale, they can be found in Sicilian pastry shops year-round. Both the dough and the sweet cheese filling are scented with the lemon and orange, making this a feast for your senses as you bite into the fragrant, flaky fried pastry. Cinnamon and chocolate chips are also included to make this a truly decadent dessert. The scraps after cutting out the rounds can be fried and sugared as a lovely chef's snack!

MAKES
12 hand pies

FILLING

1 cup whole-milk ricotta

¾ cup mascarpone cheese

1 large egg

3 tablespoons confectioners' sugar

Zest of ½ lemon

Zest of ½ large navel orange

1 teaspoon ground cinnamon

¾ cup mini chocolate chips

DOUGH

3¼ cups (390 grams) all-purpose flour, plus more for dusting

¼ cup (50 grams) granulated sugar

Zest of 1 lemon

Zest of ½ large navel orange

2 large eggs

2 tablespoons Marsala wine or brandy

1 tablespoon extra-virgin olive oil

TO ASSEMBLE

1 large egg, beaten with 1 tablespoon water, for egg wash

4 cups neutral oil, such as canola or grapeseed, for frying

½ cup confectioners' sugar

◆ Place the ricotta in a fine-mesh sieve set over a bowl. Cover and refrigerate overnight to drain.

◆ MAKE THE DOUGH: In a food processor, combine the flour, granulated sugar, lemon zest, and orange zest and pulse to incorporate. With the motor running, add the eggs, wine, and olive oil and process until a soft dough forms. Add 2 tablespoons water and pulse again until the dough is soft and pliable.

◆ Transfer the dough to a lightly floured work surface and knead into a large ball. Cut the ball into four 4-ounce portions and place on a baking sheet. Cover with plastic wrap and refrigerate while you make the filling.

◆ MAKE THE FILLING: Transfer the drained ricotta to a large bowl. Add the mascarpone, egg, and confectioners' sugar and use a handheld mixer to combine. Fold in the lemon lest, orange zest, cinnamon, and chocolate chips. Set aside.

◆ Line a baking sheet with parchment paper. Roll out one of the dough balls to a ⅛-inch-thick rectangle. Using a 4-inch round cutter, cut 3 circles. If the dough springs back after cutting, use your rolling pin to reroll. Place 1 heaping tablespoon of the filling a bit off center of each round and brush the edges with egg wash. Fold the circle over and crimp the edges with a fork to seal. Place the finished pastries on the prepared baking sheet and continue with the remaining dough.

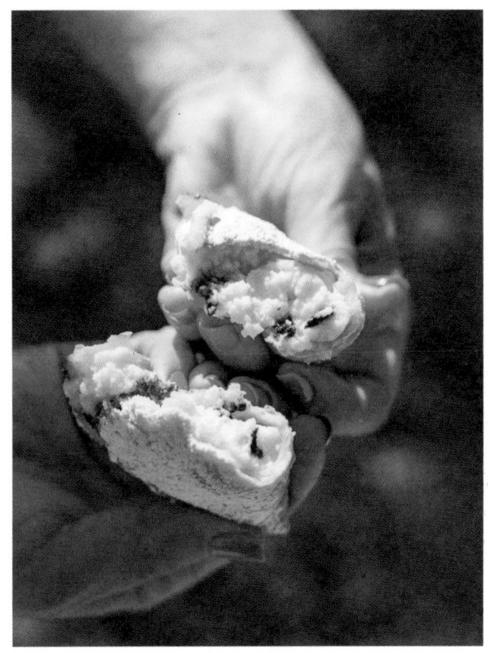

◆ In a medium Dutch oven, heat the neutral oil over medium-high heat until it reaches 350°F on a candy or deep-fry thermometer. Line a baking sheet with paper towels.

◆ Drop 3 pastries into the hot oil and fry, turning them occasionally, for 3 to 4 minutes, until they puff and begin to brown slightly. Drain on the paper towel–lined baking sheet and let cool for 10 minutes. Sift confectioners' sugar over the top and serve immediately.

Cannoli Classici

CLASSIC CANNOLI

I can't think of a more iconic Italian sweet than cannoli. These cream-filled wafers can be found throughout Italy—as well as in every Little Italy across the United States. While the regional origin of cannoli is uncertain, it is most frequently credited to Sicily. It has been said that during the island's Arab domination, in the town of Caltanissetta, this preparation was handed down from Muslim women to the Christian nuns in the area, who would make them for Carnevale. Unlike many Italian festival treats, the cannoli became so popular they are now produced year-round! They are the perfect handheld accompaniment to coffee. When no one is looking, give it a dunk.

MAKES
15 cannoli

SHELLS

1 cup all-purpose flour, plus more for dusting

¼ cup confectioners' sugar

½ teaspoon kosher salt

1 large egg, beaten

½ teaspoon ground cinnamon

¼ teaspoon unsweetened cocoa powder

2 tablespoons Marsala wine or sherry

1½ tablespoons white wine vinegar

2 tablespoons unsalted butter, at room temperature

FILLING

1 pound ricotta impastata (see Notes, page 148), at room temperature

¼ cup mascarpone cheese, at room temperature

½ to ¾ cup confectioners' sugar, to taste

1 teaspoon pure vanilla extract

1 teaspoon orange zest or orange extract (optional)

4 cups neutral oil, such as canola or grapeseed, for frying

GARNISH (OPTIONAL)

½ cup mini chocolate chips

¾ cup confectioners' sugar

SPECIAL EQUIPMENT

15 stainless-steel or wooden cannoli molds

RECIPE CONTINUES

• MAKE THE SHELLS: Place all the shell ingredients in a food processor and process until a soft dough forms, 3 to 4 minutes. (The ingredients can also be mixed in a large bowl by hand.) Transfer to a lightly floured work surface and knead until combined and smooth, about 5 minutes. Cover with plastic wrap and refrigerate for 1 hour. (The dough will be very soft.)

• MEANWHILE, MAKE THE FILLING: In a large bowl, stir together both cheeses, the confectioners' sugar, vanilla, and orange zest (if using) until well combined. Spoon the filling into a large piping bag fitted with a wide star or round tip. Set aside at room temperature while you make the shells.

• Remove the dough from the refrigerator and divide into four pieces. On a lightly floured work surface, roll out one piece of dough to ¼-inch thickness. Using a 3- or 4-inch round cutter, cut out as many disks from the dough as you can, then reroll the scraps and cut more disks. Roll each round of dough into a very thin oval shape. Sprinkle with flour as needed if the dough becomes too soft. Repeat with the remaining three pieces of dough.

• Line a baking sheet with paper towels and place the mini chocolate chips into a small bowl.

• In a medium Dutch oven, heat the neutral oil over medium-high heat until it reaches 350°F on a candy or deep-fry thermometer.

• Wrap the dough disks around the cannoli molds and use a little bit of water to seal. Working in batches, use tongs to place dough seam side down and fry until golden brown, 1 to 2 minutes. (The seams will try to release, so use a fork or tongs to press them back into place as they fry.) Once the seams are firmly attached, roll the cannoli shell to the other side and continue frying until it's golden brown, 1 to 2 minutes more. Transfer the shell to the prepared baking sheet and let cool completely. (The molds will be very hot.)

• Once cooled, carefully slip the shells off the molds and fill the shells with the cheese mixture. Press some mini chocolate chips into the filling at each end of the cannoli and sift confectioners' sugar over the shells.

NOTES

The recipe calls for ricotta impastata, *a ricotta that's double drained and whipped smooth for a creamier consistency. If you cannot find it, place the same quantity of whole-milk ricotta in a fine-mesh sieve set over a bowl and let the excess liquid drain overnight in the fridge.*

If prepping for a party, make the cannoli shells in advance and keep the filling in a piping bag in the fridge. About a half hour before serving, pull the filling from the fridge to come to room temperature. Fill and garnish the cannoli right before serving.

Coca-Cola
Coca

Bomboloni

CUSTARD-FILLED DOUGHNUTS

Bomboloni are pillowy doughnuts filled with pastry cream. The word *bombolone* is associated with the word *bomba*, which means "bomb" in Italian, as they resemble a grenade! While they are thought to have originated in Tuscany, you can find them all over Italy. They are a bit labor-intensive, so I usually make the custards the day before. That way, they're chilled for when the bomboloni are fried and ready to fill. Because I can never choose between vanilla or chocolate filling, so I make a double batch and have both. (To do the same, melt ¾ cup dark chocolate and stir it into the vanilla custard.)

MAKES
about 20 doughnuts

¾ cup warm whole milk (110°F)

½ cup sugar

1 (¼-ounce) packet active dry yeast (2¼ teaspoons)

1½ cups 00 flour, plus more for dusting

1 cup bread flour

2 large eggs, at room temperature, beaten

Zest of 1 lemon

1 teaspoon kosher salt

5 tablespoons unsalted butter, at room temperature

2 teaspoons extra-virgin olive oil, plus more for greasing

4 cups sunflower oil or other neutral oil, for frying

Vanilla Custard Filling (see page 45)

- In a small bowl, whisk together the milk, sugar, and yeast. Let stand for 5 minutes.

- In the bowl of a stand mixer fitted with the dough hook, combine both flours, the eggs, lemon zest, and salt. With the mixer on medium-low speed, add the milk mixture and beat until just combined.

- Transfer the dough to a lightly floured work surface and begin to knead. Slowly drop pieces of the butter into the dough, kneading them in until the butter dissolves into the dough before adding more. This should take about 15 minutes.

- Grease a large bowl with olive oil, place the dough in the bowl, and cover with a kitchen towel. Let the dough rise in a warm spot for 2 hours.

- Line a baking sheet with parchment. Remove the dough from the bowl and divide it into 20 equal-size balls, rolling them as you go. Place the dough balls on the prepared baking sheet, leaving 2 inches between each, then cover and let proof in a warm spot for 1 hour, until almost doubled in size.

- During the last 20 minutes of proofing, in a medium Dutch oven, heat the sunflower oil over medium-high heat until it reaches 350°F on a candy or deep-fry thermometer. Line a baking sheet with paper towels.

- Working in batches, use your hands to carefully drop 2 or 3 bomboloni into the hot oil. Fry for 2 minutes, until puffed. Flip and fry for 2 minutes more. Transfer to the prepared baking sheet and repeat with remaining bomboloni.

◆ When the bomboloni are completely cooled, cut a small slit into the side of each. Fit a large piping bag with a ¼-inch round tip and fill with the custard. Insert the tip into the side of a bombolone and pipe in the custard until the doughnut gets plump and a bit of the custard begins to peek out. Repeat to fill the remaining bomboloni.

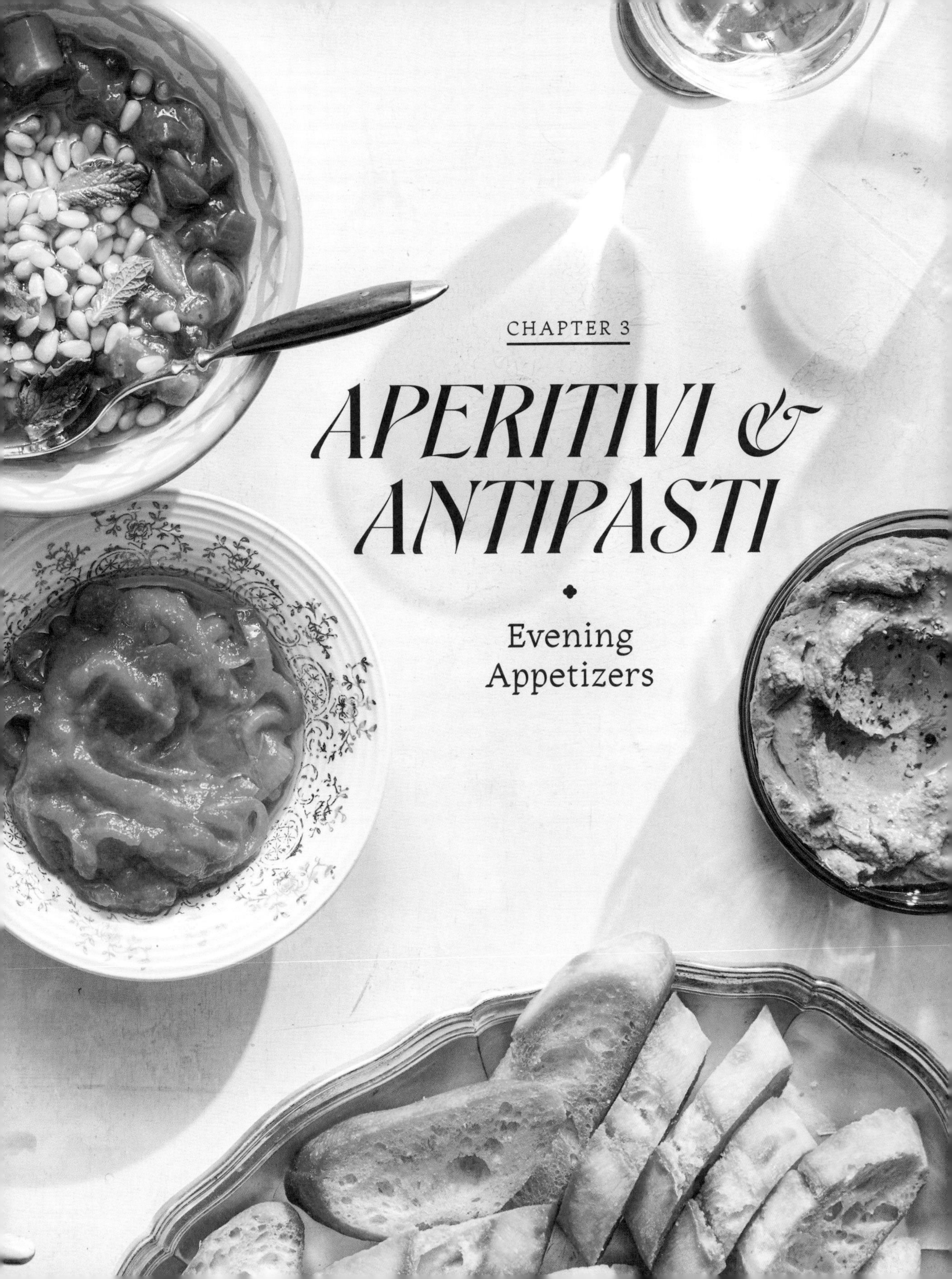

CHAPTER 3

APERITIVI & ANTIPASTI

Evening Appetizers

Crostini

TOASTED BREAD POINTS

The word *crostini* means "little crusts" in Italian. Small pieces of round sliced bread are toasted and used as a vehicle for several delicious toppings. What I love about crostini is, based on the region you are in, the crostini topping will be specific to the area's favorite ingredient combinations. I love making them in the oven, but they also taste delicious fried in a cast-iron skillet.

MAKES
14 crostini

1 (16-inch) baguette

¼ cup extra-virgin olive oil

1 teaspoon kosher salt

- Place a 9 × 13-inch baking sheet in the oven and preheat the oven to 350°F.
- Cut the baguette into 1-inch slices (save the ends for making the Cheesy Breadcrumbs on page 267).
- Once the oven is preheated, remove the hot pan and pour the oil onto it. Sprinkle the salt over the oil. Using a pastry brush, brush the salty oil on one side of the bread slices and place on the baking sheet, unoiled-side down.
- Bake on the top rack of the oven for 10 minutes, until golden brown. Remove from the oven and let cool before adding the toppings of your choice.

Peperonata

STEWED SWEET PEPPERS

This stewed pepper dish, perfect for an afternoon *spuntino*, served with a cold glass of wine, was one my grandmother made quite often, with vegetables picked from her garden. The ingredients are cooked slowly with high-quality olive oil, and the vegetables get soft enough to spread over grilled bread. My mother makes it every summer and discovered it tastes quite good with grilled meats. Funnily enough, we love it on top of hot dogs, as it's better than any store-bought relish. This chunky spread is versatile and keeps in the refrigerator for weeks.

MAKES
5½ cups

¼ cup extra-virgin olive oil, plus more as needed

5 bell peppers (any color, but a mix of red, yellow, and orange is pretty), seeded and thinly sliced

1 large red onion, thinly sliced

1 teaspoon dried oregano

2 pounds ripe tomatoes, seeded and cut into 1-inch dice

3 garlic cloves, thinly sliced

2 teaspoons kosher salt

1 teaspoon crushed red pepper flakes, to taste (optional)

1 teaspoon red wine vinegar

⅓ cup fresh basil leaves, torn

Crostini (page 154), for serving

◆ In a large high-sided skillet, heat the oil over medium heat. Add the bell peppers and onion to the skillet. Add the oregano and stir well. Cook, stirring occasionally, until the peppers start to soften, about 10 minutes.

◆ Add the tomatoes, garlic, salt, and red pepper flakes (if using). Reduce the heat to low, cover, and cook, stirring occasionally, until the tomatoes are softened, about 10 minutes. Stir in the vinegar and remove from the heat.

◆ Stir in the basil leaves and finish with a light drizzle of oil. Serve with crostini.

Pate di Olive

WHIPPED OLIVE SPREAD

With more than 60 million olive trees, brought to the region by the ancient Greeks back in 1000 BCE, Puglia produces almost half of Italy's olive oil. An inherent part of Pugliese culture, olives are present in many of the region's traditional recipes, and are also cured in their own oil. I love eating oil-cured olives with bread and cheese, or pureeing them into this spread to serve on crostini. If you cannot find oil-cured olives, Kalamatas (thanks again to the Greeks) are a perfect substitute. This spread can be served chunky or very smooth based on your preference.

MAKES
2½ cups

1 cup Italian oil-cured black olives or Kalamata olives, pitted

1 teaspoon kosher salt

1 anchovy fillet (optional)

1 teaspoon dried oregano

¼ cup extra-virgin olive oil

Crostini (page 154), for serving

- In a food processor, combine the olives, salt, anchovy (if using), oregano, and oil and pulse to your desired consistency.

- Serve with crostini. Transfer leftovers to a jar with a tight-fitting lid and store in the refrigerator for up to 1 month.

Friggione

BOLOGNESE TOMATO ONION JAM

This braised tomato sauce is simple to make and has many uses. On the street, you can buy it in a small paper dish, served with crostini for dipping and spreading; at home, it is used as a pasta sauce or garnish. Like many traditional Italian dishes that have survived the centuries (this dish was created in the 1800s), it is registered at the Bologna Chamber of Commerce. Initially, the sauce was made with lard, but extra-virgin olive oil is more commonly used today. The addition of crushed red pepper flakes is another traditional version.

While it takes a bit of time, the jam itself is simple. Onions are macerated to soften but produce an *agrodolce*, a sweet yet sour liquid that accumulates at the bottom of the bowl. This liquid is added to the sauce to create balance and reduce acidity. The jam lasts a few weeks in the fridge; after having it on bread, try it as a condiment on meat or fish. My family makes it extra spicy in the summer during tomato season. We have it on the table whenever we are barbecuing as it tastes wonderful on meats.

MAKES
4 cups

2 pounds white onions, thinly sliced

1 tablespoon kosher salt, plus more to taste

1 teaspoon sugar

3 tablespoons extra-virgin olive oil

1 teaspoon crushed red pepper flakes (optional)

1 (28-ounce) can crushed tomatoes

1 teaspoon freshly ground black pepper

Crostini (page 154), for serving

◆ In a large glass bowl, combine the onions, 1 tablespoon of the salt, and the sugar, tossing with a large spoon or tongs to evenly coat. Let the onions sit at room temperature for 4 hours, tossing them every 25 to 30 minutes.

◆ When the onions have macerated, in a large Dutch oven, heat the oil over medium heat. Add the onions and all the liquid that has accumulated in the bowl.

◆ Cook the onions, stirring occasionally, for 7 to 10 minutes. The onions should become very soft but not brown. If they begin to brown, reduce the heat. Add the red pepper flakes (if using) and give the onions one more stir.

◆ Add the tomatoes, then fill the can with water, give it a swish, and add the water to the pot as well. Stir to combine. Raise the heat to medium-high to bring the mixture to a boil, then reduce the heat to low and simmer, partially covered, stirring occasionally to prevent the onions from sticking to the bottom of the pot, for 2 hours, then remove from the heat.

◆ Add the pepper and season to taste with more salt. Serve with the crostini.

Fegatini di Pollo

CHICKEN LIVER PÂTÉ

Chicken liver pâté is the signature crostini spread of Tuscany. You will find it on most restaurant menus as an antipasto. The anchovies and capers add umami while the wine and chicken broth aid in creating a creamy consistency. This is the perfect make-ahead bite, as the flavors continue to develop after a day or two. Simply bring the spread to room temperature before spreading on the toasts.

MAKES
1¾ cups

- 2 tablespoons extra-virgin olive oil
- 2 anchovy fillets, packed in oil
- 1 small onion, minced
- 1 pound chicken livers, rinsed and veins removed
- 2 teaspoons capers
- ½ cup white wine
- ½ cup chicken broth
- 2 teaspoons kosher salt
- 1 teaspoon freshly ground black pepper
- Crostini (page 154), for serving

◆ In a large sauté pan, heat the oil over medium heat. Add the anchovies and press them into the oil to break them up. Add the onion and stir to combine. Cook until translucent, 5 to 7 minutes.

◆ Raise the heat to high and add the livers. Cook until the livers easily release from the pan, 3 minutes. Reduce the heat to medium and cook, stirring frequently, until the livers are cooked through and no longer pink, 2 minutes. Add the capers and cook for 7 minutes more.

◆ Raise the heat to high and add the wine. Cook until the wine has almost evaporated, about 5 minutes. Add the broth and cook until the liquid has reduced by half, 5 minutes more. Stir in the salt and pepper. Remove from the heat and set aside to cool, about 10 minutes.

◆ Transfer the mixture to a food processor and pulse until the desired consistency (either entirely smooth or retaining some texture, depending on your preference) is achieved. Spread on crostini and serve immediately.

Baccalà Mantecato

WHIPPED SALTED COD SPREAD

In Venice, you simply cannot enjoy drinks and *cicchetti* without including a platter of crostini generously topped with *baccalà mantecato.* While it is truly the Venetians' signature snack, the baccalà prepared in Venice comes from the shores of Norway. The fish is dried and salted, a historic method of preserving fish that dates back to the days before refrigeration. To "revive" the fish, it is soaked for five days, with the water getting changed daily to assist in removing most of the salt. Traditionally, the fish is beaten by hand into a paste, but a food processor does the job nicely. Many Italian Americans also eat baccalà for Christmas Eve; your fishmonger will have plenty around the holidays.

MAKES
3 cups

1 pound salted cod

1 cup whole milk

¼ cup extra-virgin olive oil

Crostini (page 154), for serving

◆ Place the cod in a container and add water to cover completely. Refrigerate the fish for 5 days, changing the water once a day. On day 6, remove the fish from the water and cut it into 2-inch pieces.

◆ In a medium saucepan, combine the fish and the milk and bring to a boil. Reduce the heat to low and simmer for 15 minutes, until the fish begins to break apart easily with a fork. Reserve ½ cup of the milk, then drain the fish.

◆ In a food processor, combine the fish and the reserved milk. With the motor running, pour the oil in and process until creamy.

◆ Spread the mantecato on crostini and serve at room temperature. Store leftovers in an airtight container in the refrigerator for up to 1 week; bring back to room temperature before serving.

Caponata

STEWED EGGPLANT SPREAD

Caponata is an *agrodolce* (see page 158) cooked salad where eggplant is the star. You'll find this spreadable, saucy veggie dish throughout Sicily, with slight variations in every nonna's pot. It is the perfect antipasto, served with bread to sop up the oily tomato-based sauce. Each ingredient plays a part in this sweet yet tart spread. Capers, olives, vinegar, and tomatoes add acid and bite, while the raisins and sugar balance the punch with a candied quality. Eggplant, nature's sponge, soaks up all the flavors and infuses them into the bread when spread on with the back of a spoon. While the nonnas usually cook all the ingredients in a large pot, I like to prebake my eggplant to avoid excess oil absorption.

MAKES
6 cups

½ cup extra-virgin olive oil, plus more for drizzling

3 or 4 Italian eggplants (about 1½ pounds)

1 medium red onion, cut into small dice (about 1 cup)

2 celery stalks, cut into small dice (about 1 cup)

½ teaspoon kosher salt, plus more to taste

½ teaspoon freshly ground black pepper, plus more to taste

1 teaspoon crushed red pepper flakes (optional)

2 garlic cloves, thinly sliced

½ cup red wine vinegar

1 tablespoon tomato paste

⅔ cup canned tomato sauce

1 teaspoon sugar

1 cup chicken stock

1 tablespoon capers, drained

¼ cup Castelvetrano olives, pitted and coarsely chopped

¼ cup raisins

Chopped fresh mint leaves, for serving

Toasted pine nuts, for serving

Crostini (page 154) or cooked couscous, for serving

◆ Drizzle ¼ cup of the oil into a 9 × 13-inch baking pan. Place the pan in the oven and preheat the oven to 350°F.

◆ Peel the eggplants and cut off their tops. Dice the flesh into 1-inch pieces. Remove the hot pan from the oven and toss the eggplant with the warmed oil. Spread the eggplant in an even layer over the pan and bake for 10 minutes, until the eggplant is soft and beginning to brown.

◆ Meanwhile, heat the remaining ¼ cup oil in a large sauté pan over medium heat. Add the onion, celery, salt, black pepper, and red pepper flakes (if using) and cook, stirring frequently, until the onion is translucent, about 5 minutes. Add the garlic and cook until softened and the onions have begun to caramelize, 2 minutes more. Stir in the vinegar.

◆ Add the tomato paste and press it into the hot pan with a metal spatula. It will begin to blend with the ingredients and break up. Allow the vinegar to reduce by half, about 2 minutes. Add the tomato sauce, sugar, and stock, stirring to incorporate. Raise the heat to medium-high and bring the sauce to a boil.

◆ Add the roasted eggplant to the pan. Stir everything together, folding the sauce over the eggplant. Reduce the heat to medium and add the capers, olives, and raisins. Stir again, cover, and cook, stirring frequently to prevent sticking, for 15 minutes. (Reduce the heat if stirring doesn't prevent sticking.)

◆ Remove from the heat and add the mint and pine nuts. Season with more salt and black pepper to taste. Transfer to a serving bowl and drizzle with oil. Serve warm or at room temperature, on crostini or over couscous. Store leftovers in an airtight container in the refrigerator for up to 1 week; rewarm or bring to room temperature before serving.

Grissini

BLACK PEPPER BREADSTICKS

One of my favorites things about Italy is the custom of nibbling while drinking predinner cocktails. While out for *aperitivi*, I am always excited for the little dishes of olives, nuts, and crunchy breadsticks the waiter brings to the table. Drinking pairs with salty, carby snacks. One bread I can't resist is grissini. Originally from Turin, this leavened breadstick is a handheld crunchy treat, usually paired with cured meats and cheeses. My mother always made them with lots of black pepper, giving them a spicy kick. Grissini pair perfectly with hard cheeses and salty salumi.

MAKES
48 sticks

1 (¼-ounce) packet active dry yeast (2¼ teaspoons)

1¼ cups (300 grams) warm water (110°F)

½ cup (100 grams) extra-virgin olive oil, plus more for the bowl

4 cups (480 grams) all-purpose flour, plus more as needed

1½ teaspoons kosher salt

1½ teaspoons freshly ground black pepper

2 teaspoons aniseed

1 egg yolk, beaten with 1 tablespoon water, for egg wash

- Line three baking sheets with parchment paper.
- In a small bowl, combine the yeast and ¼ cup (60 grams) of the warm water. Let stand for 5 minutes.
- In a spouted measuring cup, combine the remaining 1 cup (240 grams) warm water and the oil.
- In a large bowl, combine the flour, salt, pepper, and aniseed. Stir in the yeast mixture and the water-oil mixture to form a soft dough. (Add more flour if needed.)
- Knead the dough in the bowl until it comes together into a smooth ball, 5 to 10 minutes.
- Transfer the dough to an oiled bowl, turn to oil the surface, cover, and let rise in a warm spot until doubled in size, about 30 minutes.
- Punch down the dough, then transfer to a lightly floured work surface and press the dough into a roughly 6 × 24-inch rectangle, ½ inch thick. Cut into ½-inch-wide strips (48 total), then roll the strips into thin ropes, about ¼ inch thick and 12 inches long. Place 1 inch apart on the prepared baking sheets.
- Brush the dough ropes with the egg wash and let proof, uncovered, in a warm spot for 20 minutes.
- Preheat the oven to 400°F.
- Bake the grissini for 20 to 22 minutes, rotating the sheets halfway through, until golden brown. Let cool completely before serving. Store the grissini in an airtight container at room temperature for up to 1 week or in zip-top bags in the freezer for up to 1 month.

◆

TARALLINI

Small Round Crackers

TARALLI are *the* Italian pretzel. Found all over Southern Italy, this circular cracker as has a great crunch when you bite into it. A soft, flavored dough is rolled out to a skinny rope and then shaped into a round with one end pressed into the other.

When out for drinks, you will find that the mini version, *tarallini*, are commonly served in a small dish and presented on a platter with olives and nuts. They are ubiquitous in Italian food markets, and the flavor possibilities are endless. The perfect accompaniment to cheese and salumi, tarallini are a staple on any great antipasto platter, too. These recipes make a bunch but have no fear, they get better with age.

TARALLINI DI OLIVE (OPPOSITE TOP), PAGE 168
TARALLINI AL PEPERONCINO (OPPOSITE BOTTOM), PAGE 169

Tarallini di Olive

OLIVE TARALLINI

MAKES
about 60 tarallini

1 (¼-ounce) packet active dry yeast (2¼ teaspoons)

1 cup (240 grams) warm water (110°F)

1 cup Italian oil-cured black olives or Kalamata olives, pitted

4½ cups (540 grams) all-purpose flour, plus more for dusting

1¼ teaspoons kosher salt

½ cup (100 grams) extra-virgin olive oil

• Position racks in the middle and upper third of the oven and preheat the oven to 350°F. Line two baking sheets with parchment paper.

• In a small bowl, whisk the yeast and warm water to combine and let stand for 5 minutes.

• In a food processor, pulse the olives to form a coarse paste.

• In the bowl of a stand mixer fitted with the dough hook, combine the flour and salt. With the mixer on medium speed, add the oil and the yeasted water. Add the olive paste and mix until a shaggy dough forms.

• Transfer the dough to a clean work surface and knead until the dough is smooth and elastic, 5 to 7 minutes. If the dough is tacky, sprinkle with a bit of flour and continue kneading. Transfer the dough to a bowl, cover with plastic wrap, and let rest for 15 minutes to allow the flour to fully absorb the moisture and hydrate the dough.

• Pinch off about a tablespoon of the dough and roll it into a thin rope, about 6 inches long, with tapered ends. Bring the two ends together and press to create a small circle. Repeat with the remaining dough, placing the tarallini about 1 inch apart on the prepared baking sheets as you shape them.

• Place one baking sheet on the middle rack and bake for 10 minutes. Then move the sheet to the upper rack and bake until the tarallini are crisp and golden, 15 to 20 minutes more. When the first sheet is moved to the top rack, the second sheet can be placed on the middle rack and baked as you did the first batch. Allow the tarallini to cool completely on the baking sheets before serving or storing. Store in an airtight container in a cool, dry place for up to 1 week.

Tarallini al Peperoncino

SPICY TARALLINI

MAKES
about 60 tarallini

1 (¼-ounce) packet active dry yeast (2¼ teaspoons)

1 cup (240 grams) warm water (110°F)

½ cup (100 grams) extra-virgin olive oil

1 teaspoon paprika

4½ cups (540 grams) all-purpose flour, plus more for dusting

1 tablespoon crushed red pepper flakes

1¼ teaspoons kosher salt

- Position racks in the middle and upper third of the oven and preheat the oven to 350°F. Line two baking sheets with parchment paper.

- In a small bowl, whisk the yeast and warm water and let stand for 5 minutes. In a small bowl, whisk the oil and paprika.

- In the bowl of a stand mixer fitted with the dough hook, combine the flour, red pepper flakes, and salt. With the mixer on medium speed, add the paprika oil and the yeasted water. Mix until a shaggy dough forms.

- Transfer to a clean work surface and knead until the dough is smooth and elastic, 5 to 7 minutes. If the dough is tacky, sprinkle with a bit of flour and continue kneading. Transfer the dough to a bowl, cover with plastic wrap, and let rest for 15 minutes to allow the flour to fully absorb the moisture and hydrate the dough.

- Pinch off about a tablespoon of the dough and roll it into a thin rope, about 6 inches long, with tapered ends. Bring the two ends together and press to create a small circle. Repeat with the remaining dough, placing the tarallini about 1 inch apart on the baking sheets as you shape them.

- Place one baking sheet on the middle rack and bake for 10 minutes. Then move the sheet to the upper rack and bake until the tarallini are crisp and golden, 15 to 20 minutes more. When the first sheet is moved to the top rack, the second sheet can be placed on the middle rack and baked as you did the first batch. Allow the tarallini to cool completely on the baking sheets before serving or storing. Store in an airtight container in a cool, dry place for up to 1 week.

Bagna Càuda

ANCHOVY DIP

Bagna càuda is Italian for "hot bath." This thin, buttery, olive oil–based dip is a Piemontese classic. It's served in a fondue pot with crostini and *pinzimonio* alongside. Pinzimonio refers to serving crudités with an olive oil, salt, and pepper dipping sauce. To eat, the vegetables are dipped into the hot dip while the bread acts as the plate, catching any drippings. It's warm, rich, and salty. The addition of the anchovies (lots of them) is the Piemonte way. If you add capers and omit the butter, you'll have the Neapolitan version, called *acciugata*.

MAKES
¾ cup

- 5 garlic cloves, minced
- ¼ cup whole milk
- 1 cup extra-virgin olive oil
- 1 (3.35-ounce) jar anchovy fillets, packed in oil
- 5 tablespoons unsalted butter
- 1 teaspoon truffle oil (optional)

FOR SERVING

- Assorted raw vegetables and Crostini (page 154)

◆ In a measuring cup, combine the garlic and milk. Let steep for 1 hour. Drain the garlic and discard the milk.

◆ In a small saucepan, heat the oil over medium heat. Add the anchovies and the milk-steeped garlic. Using the back of a spatula, gently press the anchovies into the warm oil. They will begin to melt after 1 to 2 minutes.

◆ Cook until the anchovies have dissolved completely, then add the butter and truffle oil (if using).

◆ To serve, pour the sauce into a fondue pot or bowl and serve with raw vegetables and crostini.

Fonduta

FONDUE

One snowy winter, I spent some time in Cervinia skiing and enjoying the rich cuisine of the Valle d'Aosta region, high up in the Italian Alps. Fonduta, a thick cheese sauce made with their very special Fontina cheese, is served in many restaurants, tableside, with a large platter of vegetables, meats, and cheese for dipping. It is also poured on top of polenta for a very filling side dish. Perfect after a day on the slopes.

MAKES
3 cups

¾ cup heavy cream

¼ cup whole milk

1 pound Fontina cheese, shredded

4 tablespoons (57 grams) unsalted butter

5 egg yolks, beaten

1 teaspoon kosher salt

FOR SERVING

Assorted raw vegetables, apple slices, and Crostini (page 154)

- In a medium saucepan, combine the cream and milk and heat over low heat. When the milk begins to bubble, add the Fontina and stir until the cheese begins to melt, about 3 minutes. Add the butter and stir to melt.

- Vigorously whisk a spoonful of the cheese sauce into the egg yolks. Slowly drizzle the egg yolk mixture into the saucepan, whisking continuously to prevent the yolks from separating. Whisk in the salt.

- Cook the sauce over very low heat, stirring occasionally, for 5 minutes. Transfer the fonduta to a fondue pot and serve with vegetable, apples, and crostini.

Tramezzini

ITALIAN TEA SANDWICHES

These sandwiches, created by a chef at Caffè Mulassano in Torino, date back to 1925. *Tramezzino* combines *tra* ("in between") and *mezzo* ("half"), which refers to the fillings and how the sandwiches are sliced. The bread is a white Pullman loaf, called *pan carrè*, a French-Italian hybrid, which is spread with some good aioli (see page 266) before the fillings are added. Since their creation, the tradition has been to serve these dainty sandwiches as an after-work snack for hungry commuters. Always served with a glass of wine or aperitivo, these are also "entertaining" sandwiches for get-togethers. As they are available most of the day, a few can also serve as a perfect lunch for those needing something on the go. Here are some variations from my memories of eating these fun, crustless sandwiches with so many lovely fillings on the Venetian Grand Canal.

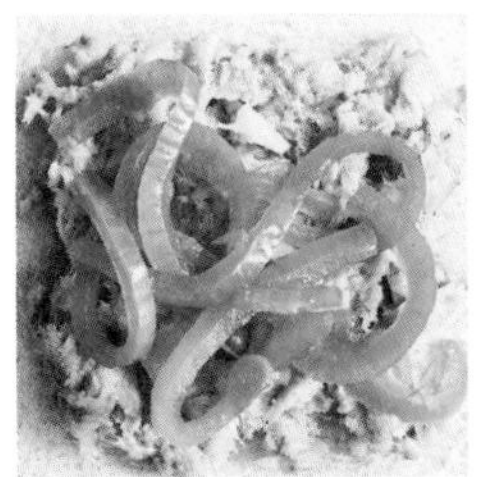

THE RIALTO

Pickled Red Onion (see page 265)
Italian Tuna Salad (page 177)
Arugula

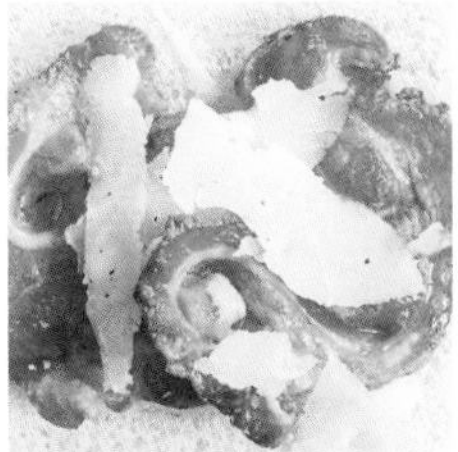

THE BACON, EGG, AND CHEESE

Hard-boiled egg, sliced
Crisp pancetta
Shaved Pecorino Romano

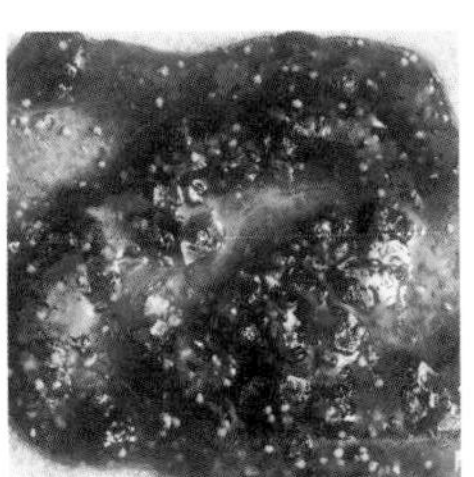

THE SALATA DOLCE

Fig jam
Prosciutto
Flaky sea salt

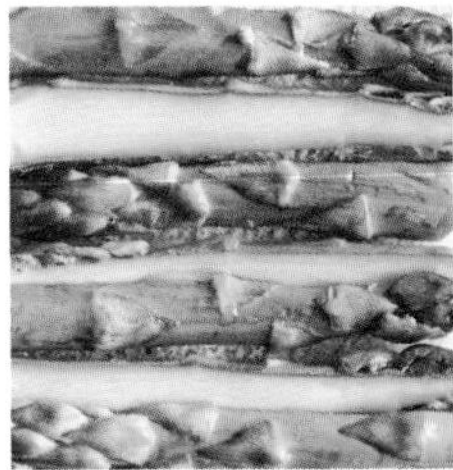

THE BRUNCH

Hard-boiled egg, chopped
Steamed asparagus

CONTINUES

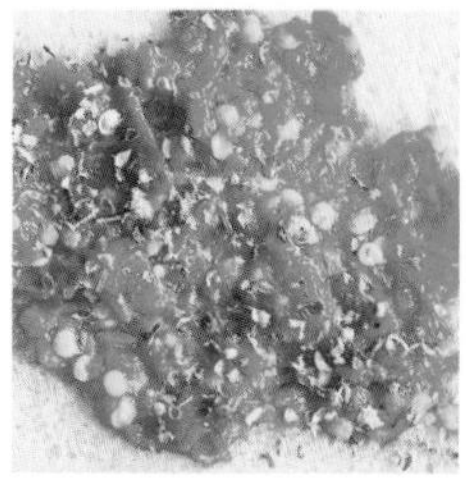

THE FOREST FIRE

Sautéed mushrooms

Dried oregano

Calabrian chile paste

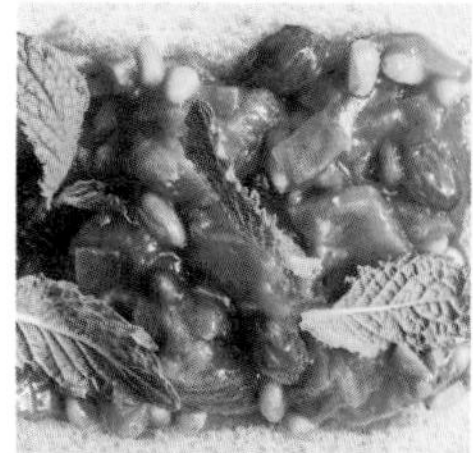
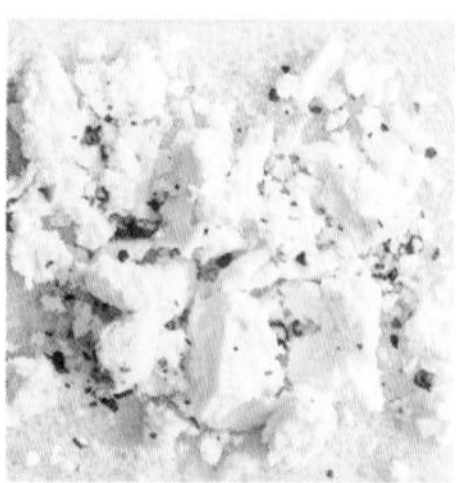

THE NORMA

Caponata (page 162)

Ricotta salata

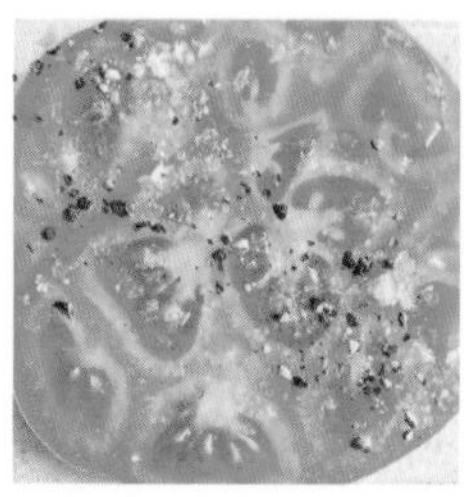

THE HOLY TRINITY

Fresh mozzarella

Basil

Tomato

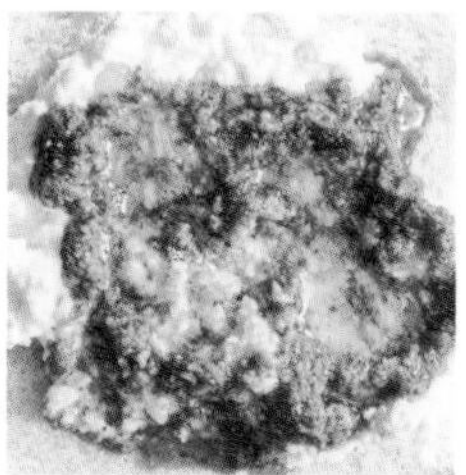

THE PIGS IN A BLANKET

Mortadella

Ricotta

Perfect Pesto (see page 267)

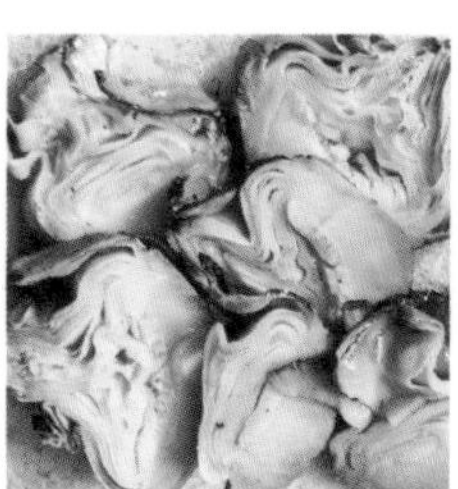

THE HEARTBREAKER

Jarred marinated artichoke hearts

Salami

Arugula

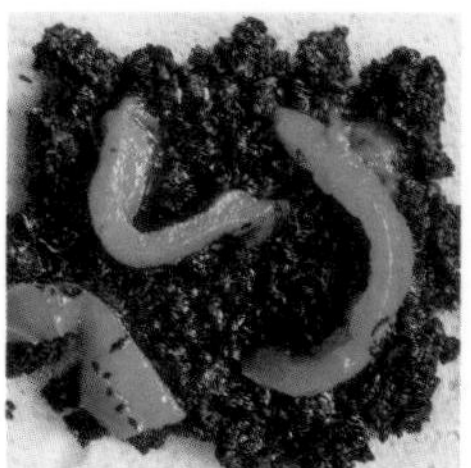

THE MUD RUCKER

Olive spread (see page 157)

Capicola (a sliced Italian deli meat) or Genoa salami

Roasted red peppers

Arugula

Insalata di Tonno

ITALIAN TUNA SALAD

Oil-packed tuna is a pantry staple in Italy. The large fillets can be found jarred or tinned in olive or sunflower oil. I love the way the oil softens the tuna as it sits in the jar. Adding punchy flavors like capers and lemon make this salad so bright. Perfectly spreadable, this tuna makes an ideal sandwich filling.

MAKES
about 3 cups

2 (6- to 7-ounce) jars tuna fillets, packed in olive oil (about 1½ cups)

5 or 6 marinated artichokes, drained

1 tablespoon capers, drained

Juice of ½ lemon

1 teaspoon kosher salt, plus more to taste

1 teaspoon freshly ground black pepper

1 teaspoon dried oregano

◆ In a food processor, combine all the ingredients, including the oil from the tuna jars, and pulse until your desired consistency is achieved. Taste and season with more salt if needed.

Frico Morbido

CHEESE-STUFFED POTATO PANCAKES

If you like potato latkes, you will love *frico*, a Friulian dish, specifically from Carnia, the northeastern region of Friuli. A grated potato cake traditionally stuffed with Montasio cheese fried to a crispy exterior and a soft, cheesy center, frico has peasant origins and is revered by locals for its simple preparation with super tasty results. As with most recipes, each home has its own version, some making one large pie and slicing it into pieces while others make small, snackable patties.

Make sure to use a nonstick or seasoned cast-iron skillet, so the potato patties quickly release from the pan. In addition, use a salad spinner to remove as much water as possible from the grated potato before forming the fricos. Using high-starch russet potatoes ensures a golden and crispy exterior and a fluffy interior. If you can find Montasio cheese, give it a try, but Asiago or mozzarella are worthy substitutes if you can't. They're the perfect handheld snack, but give them a few minutes to cool, so you don't end up with burnt fingers!

MAKES
about 16 frico

3 large potatoes (2 pounds), such as russets, peeled

1 medium onion

1 large egg, beaten

3 tablespoons all-purpose flour, plus more if needed

1 tablespoon kosher salt

½ teaspoon freshly ground black pepper

1 cup grated Asiago or mozzarella cheese (about 4 ounces)

¼ cup neutral oil, such as canola or grapeseed, for frying

3 tablespoons unsalted butter

- Preheat the oven to 200°F.

- On the large holes of a box grater or in a food processor using the grating disk, grate the potatoes and onion. Working in batches, spin the potatoes and onion in a salad spinner to remove all excess water. Alternatively, wrap the potatoes and onion in cheesecloth or a clean kitchen towel and squeeze out the excess water.

- In a large bowl, combine the potatoes and onion, beaten egg, flour, salt, and pepper and stir to incorporate. If the mixture is still watery, add another tablespoon of flour.

- Scoop 2 tablespoons of the potato mixture onto a clean work surface. Press a few pinches of cheese on top. Add another tablespoon of the potato mixture on top of the cheese and press to cover the cheese while forming the mixture into a patty.

- Line a baking sheet with paper towels and set a wire rack on top. In a large cast-iron skillet, heat the oil and butter over medium heat until the butter melts and the oil is hot. Carefully drop 5 or 6 patties into the hot oil. Fry for 3 to 4 minutes, until the bottom is golden brown, then flip and cook for 3 to 4 minutes more on the other side. Transfer the frico to the prepared baking sheet and place in the oven to keep warm. Repeat with the remaining patties. Serve immediately.

LE CREUSET

Rafanata

FRIED POTATO FRITTATA

This is the Italian version of the Spanish *tortilla de patatas*. In Basilicata, they add freshly grated horseradish *rafana* to this simple frittata. The potatoes are parcooked, allowing them to truly melt into the eggs once added to the pan. The frittata tastes wonderful hot, but Italians are known to slice and serve it at room temperature with a cocktail or wine. If you are skeptical about the addition of horseradish, start with a tablespoon. I promise, you will be adding more when you make this dish the next time (and the next!) for a stunning aperitivo hour.

SERVES
8

1¼ pounds Yukon Gold potatoes (about 3), peeled

2 teaspoons kosher salt

¼ cup extra-virgin olive oil

1 medium onion, thinly sliced (about 1 cup)

10 large eggs

3 tablespoons prepared horseradish

⅔ cup grated Pecorino Romano cheese (1 ounce)

- Preheat the oven to 350°F.

- Place the potatoes in a medium pot, cover with cold water, and bring to a boil over high heat. Add 1 teaspoon of the salt and cook for 10 minutes. The potatoes will not be cooked all the way through. Drain the potatoes, let cool a bit, then cut them into thin rounds.

- In a large high-sided oven-safe skillet (preferably a 12-inch nonstick), heat the oil over high heat. Arrange the potatoes and onion in the pan in a few even layers. Reduce the heat to medium and cook until the potatoes and onion begin to soften, 5 to 7 minutes. Carefully flip the layers to encourage even cooking. Reduce the heat to low and turn the potatoes every few minutes until they are tender when pierced with a fork but not brown, about 3 minutes.

- While the potatoes cook, in a medium bowl, beat the eggs. Add the horseradish and remaining 1 teaspoon salt and stir to combine. Carefully pour the egg mixture into the pan, swirling it evenly over the potatoes and onions to the edge of the pan. Cook until the eggs begin to set, about 5 minutes.

- Run a rubber spatula around the edges of the frittata to release it from the sides of the pan. Tilt the pan to allow the raw egg from the top to run down the sides of the cooked edges.

- Turn off the heat and sprinkle ⅓ cup of the pecorino evenly over the frittata. The top will still be runny. Transfer to the oven and bake the frittata for 10 minutes, until the eggs are cooked through and puffed on top.

- Slide the frittata onto a cutting board or serving platter and cut into 8 wedges. Sprinkle with the remaining pecorino. Serve warm or at room temperature.

Polpettini

BAKED MINI MEATBALLS

Every Southern Italian household has a meatball recipe; ours is from my mother. One summer, I was hosting a dinner party and wanted something bite-size to serve with predinner cocktails. I decided to change up the old faithful to truly spectacular results. I took my mother's recipe but rolled the meatballs very small, added a crumb coating, and baked them. They are so good and very poppable. Serve them with toothpicks and drinks. Just don't forget the marinara dipping sauce.

MAKES
142 polpettini

MEATBALLS

½ pound ground beef

½ pound ground pork

½ pound ground veal

1 tablespoon chopped fresh flat-leaf parsley

2 teaspoons kosher salt

1 teaspoon freshly ground black pepper

2 large eggs, beaten

½ cup grated Pecorino Romano cheese

1 cup plain breadcrumbs

½ cup whole milk

½ cup Quick Marinara Sauce (see page 265) or Gina's Tomato Sauce (see page 264), warmed

COATING

½ cup Cheesy Breadcrumbs (see page 267) or seasoned Italian breadcrumbs

½ cup grated Pecorino Romano cheese

- Preheat the oven to 350°F. Line three baking sheets with parchment paper.
- In a large bowl, combine the three meats, the parsley, salt, pepper, eggs, pecorino, breadcrumbs, and milk and mix with your hands to combine. (The hand-mixing helps prevent overmixing.) Roll into small balls, about 1½ teaspoons each.
- In a large shallow dish, combine the cheesy breadcrumbs and pecorino. Drop the meatballs, a few at a time, into the mixture and rotate the dish in a circular motion to roll the meatballs and coat with the breadcrumbs. Divide the meatballs among the prepared baking sheets.
- Bake for 6 minutes. Remove the baking sheets from the oven and gently shimmy the pans to turn the meatballs. Return to the oven and bake for 6 minutes more. Let cool slightly and serve with tomato sauce on the side for dipping.

NOTE

This recipe makes a lot of meatballs. Freeze whatever you don't think you'll use prior to baking. Store them in zip-top bags in the freezer. They'll keep for up to 1 month. I love throwing them into soup or into a baked pasta dish as well!

Polpette di Tonno

TUNA MEATBALLS

There are so many *cicchetterias* throughout Venice, but I have to say, my favorite was H2 NO. They had a glass case filled with rows and rows of savory snacks, like *tramezzini*, Venetian finger sandwiches (see pages 175–176), and these flavorful fish balls. Each cicchetti is a few euro so you fill up a platter, grab a cold beer, and enjoy the bites.

Made with olive oil–packed tuna, which is pricey but well worth the expense, a little bit of potato, and breadcrumbs, they come together quickly and pair wonderfully with my simple lemony aioli.

MAKES
24 meatballs

1 large potato (about 8 ounces), peeled

2 (7-ounce) jars tuna packed in olive oil

Zest and juice of 1 lemon

1 large egg, beaten

¾ cup breadcrumbs

½ cup extra-virgin olive oil

Italian Aioli (see page 266), for serving

- Place the potato in a small pot and add enough cold water to cover. Bring to a boil over high heat. Cook until the potato is fork-tender, 7 to 10 minutes. Drain and transfer to a plate.

- In a large bowl, combine the tuna and 1 tablespoon of the oil from the jar. Using a potato ricer, press the potato into the bowl, along with the lemon zest, lemon juice, egg, and ¼ cup of the breadcrumbs. Stir to incorporate.

- Place the remaining ½ cup breadcrumbs in a shallow bowl. Pinch off heaping tablespoons of the mixture and roll into balls. Drop the balls into the breadcrumbs and turn to coat completely.

- In a large cast-iron skillet, heat the oil over medium heat. In batches, cook the tuna balls until golden brown, 2 to 3 minutes per side. Transfer to a plate to drain and repeat to fry the remaining tuna balls.

- Serve immediately or at room temperature, with aioli on the side.

Polpette di Melanzane *alla Norma*

EGGPLANT MEATBALLS

In the south of Italy, eggplants show up in many dishes, in many variations. In Puglia, eggplant meatballs are popular, with each home making them their own, using different cheeses, sometimes capers, even chopped olives. I decided to give my eggplant polpette my own flair as well. Even if you aren't an eggplant lover, I beg you to try this recipe. The eggplant melts in the middle and gets perfectly brown crispy edges. As *pasta alla Norma* is one of my absolute favorite dishes from Sicily, I added ricotta salata and serve it with tomato sauce.

MAKES
30 meatballs

3 large eggplants, peeled and quartered

3 tablespoons finely chopped fresh flat-leaf parsley

1½ cups Cheesy Breadcrumbs (see page 267) or store-bought breadcrumbs

¾ cup grated ricotta salata

½ cup finely grated Parmigiano Reggiano cheese

3 large eggs, beaten

2 teaspoons kosher salt

1 teaspoon freshly ground black pepper

1 cup extra-virgin olive oil

Gina's Tomato Sauce (see page 264) or Quick Tomato Sauce (see page 265)

• In a large stockpot, bring 10 cups water to a boil. Add the eggplant and press it down to submerge. Boil until the eggplant is fork-tender, about 10 minutes.

• Drain the eggplant in a colander, then place in a large bowl and add cold water to cool. Drain again and squeeze each piece to remove excess water. Mince the eggplant into a pulp.

• In a large bowl, combine the eggplant pulp, parsley, breadcrumbs, both cheeses, eggs, salt, and pepper and mix with your hands until fully incorporated.

• In a large cast-iron skillet, heat ¼ cup of the oil over medium heat. Working in batches, form the eggplant mixture into balls (each about the size of a golf ball) and place them in the skillet; do not crowd the pan. Press each ball down with a fork to flatten.

• Cook until golden brown, 6 to 7 minutes per side. Transfer to a plate and repeat with the remaining eggplant balls, adding more oil to the pan as needed between batches. (Alternatively, bake at 350°F for 40 minutes.) Serve hot or at room temperature, with tomato sauce.

Melanzane Ripieni

STUFFED EGGPLANTS

Versions of stuffed eggplant can be found all over the world. My mother has been making her Calabrese version, passed down from her mother, Grazia, for as long as I can remember. What I love about this recipe is how symbolic it is of the Italian cooking method: only a few ingredients and no waste. The eggplants are scooped out and the "shells" are stuffed with the pulp and a few other meaty bits and cheese to create a rich and savory filling.

My mother bakes them (instead of the traditional frying method of her mother) for an easier-to-prepare and lighter meal. From mother to daughter, recipes evolve, but the results remain delicious.

MAKES
24 stuffed eggplants

2 tablespoons extra-virgin olive oil, plus more as needed

12 small eggplants, such as Japanese eggplant

4 ounces pancetta

1 small onion, minced

1 garlic clove, minced

½ teaspoon kosher salt

½ teaspoon freshly cracked black pepper

8 ounces ground pork

1 cup finely grated Parmigiano Reggiano cheese, plus more for finishing

½ cup Italian-seasoned breadcrumbs (not panko)

1 large egg, beaten

2 tablespoons fresh flat-leaf parsley, chopped, plus more for garnish

- Preheat the oven to 350°F. Brush a baking sheet with olive oil.

- Bring a large pot of water to a boil.

- Remove the stems from the eggplants and cut them in half lengthwise. Using a paring knife, cut a crosshatch pattern into the flesh of the eggplant, being careful not to cut through the skin. Then cut along the perimeter where the flesh meets the skin.

- Place the eggplants in the boiling water, cut-side down, and press them into the water with a large spoon to submerge. Boil for 15 minutes.

- Meanwhile, in a large sauté pan, heat the oil over medium heat. Add the pancetta and cook until crisp and the fat has rendered, 5 minutes. Add the onion, garlic, salt, and pepper and reduce the heat to low. Cook until the onion is translucent, 3 to 4 minutes.

RECIPE CONTINUES

• Add the pork and cook, breaking it up with a spatula and stirring it into the pancetta mixture, until the pork is no longer pink, about 5 minutes.

• Drain the eggplant and rinse it with cold water. Using a small spoon, scoop the pulp into a bowl, then squeeze the skins once empty to remove any excess water, then set aside. Working in batches, squeeze the pulp as well to remove excess water, then transfer to a food processor and pulse three or four times, until the pulp is finely minced.

• Add the pulp to the pork mixture and stir to combine, allowing the pulp to absorb all the flavors of the pan. Transfer to a large bowl and allow the mixture to cool.

• Add the cheese, breadcrumbs, egg, and parsley. Stir to combine.

• Spoon the filling into the eggplant skins and press down to flatten. Place them skin-side down on the prepared baking sheet. Drizzle a bit of olive oil over each filled eggplant. Bake for 10 minutes. Remove them from the oven and flip the eggplants skin-side up. Bake for 7 to 10 minutes more, until the filling is golden brown.

• Garnish with fresh parsley and grated Parmigiano, if desired. Serve immediately or at room temperature.

Olive all'Ascolana

STUFFED OLIVES

These little bites are the perfect bar snack and should be served with your favorite aperitivo. Originally developed in the Ascoli Piceno region of Le Marche in 1800 to make good use of leftovers from large celebrations, this dish is now served in many bars. In Le Marche, they are possibly the most famous dish. At festivals, they are made street-side and served in paper cones. They are traditionally made with a green variety of olive called Ascolana Tenera, but you can use any large, brine-cured green olive. Make sure to get pitted olives to avoid the painstaking method of cutting the olive off the pit in a spiral, as they do in Italy.

The glorious combination of brine from the olives, heartiness from the meat stuffing, and fat from the quick fry makes it quite impossible to eat just one—especially if you wash it down with a chilled glass of Verdicchio, a crisp white wine from Le Marche.

MAKES
150 olives

FILLING

½ small onion, cut into 1-inch pieces

1 celery stalk, trimmed and cut into 1-inch pieces

1 small carrot, cut into 1-inch pieces

1 tablespoon extra-virgin olive oil

¾ cup white wine

4 ounces 90% lean ground beef

4 ounces ground pork

4 ounces ground chicken

1 teaspoon kosher salt

1 pound pitted Ascolana olives or any large green olive, such as Castelvetrano, drained and rinsed

1 lemon

5 large eggs

1 cup freshly grated Parmigiano Reggiano cheese

1 teaspoon grated nutmeg (preferably freshly grated)

BREADING

½ cup all-purpose flour

1 cup Italian-seasoned breadcrumbs (not panko)

3 cups extra-virgin olive oil

RECIPE CONTINUES

• MAKE THE FILLING: In a mini food processor, pulse the onion, celery, and carrot until chopped into very small pieces. (Alternatively, chop the vegetables by hand.)

• In a large nonstick skillet, heat the oil over medium heat. Add the chopped vegetables and cook, stirring occasionally, until soft, about 7 minutes. Add the wine and stir to combine.

• Add the ground beef, pork, chicken, and salt and stir, breaking the meat into small pieces. Raise the heat to medium-high and cook, stirring occasionally, until all the meat is cooked through and the liquid has evaporated, about 15 minutes.

• While the meat cooks, cut the olives in half.

• Transfer the filling to a food processor and puree into a paste, scraping down the sides as necessary. Zest the lemon into the food processor (reserve the zested lemon for serving). Add 2 of the eggs, the Parmigiano, and the nutmeg and pulse to combine.

• Have a baking sheet or large platter nearby to hold the stuffed olives. Fill half the olive halves with a teaspoon of the meat mixture. Fit the remaining olive halves on top to reconstruct the olive shape and place them on the baking sheet.

• SET UP THE BREADING STATION: Place the flour, remaining 3 eggs, and breadcrumbs in three separate shallow dishes. Lightly beat the eggs. Roll each stuffed olive in the flour, followed by the egg, and then coat in breadcrumbs. Place the breaded olives back on the baking sheet. Refrigerate the breaded stuffed olives while the oil heats.

• In a medium Dutch oven, heat the oil over medium-high heat until it reaches 350°F on a candy or deep-fry thermometer. Line a large platter with paper towels. Working in batches, carefully drop several olives into the hot oil and move them around with a slotted spoon until they are golden on all sides, about 1 minute. Remove from the oil with the slotted spoon and transfer to the prepared platter to drain.

• Cut the zested lemon into wedges and squeeze them over the fried olives. Serve immediately. The fried olives can also be stored in a zip-top bag in the freezer for up to 1 month. To reheat, arrange on a baking sheet and bake at 350°F for 10 minutes.

Melanzane a Pullastiello

STUFFED EGGPLANT PATTIES

As you may have already gleaned already, I love eggplant. Stuffed, fried, or baked, I have always enjoyed its flavor and its ability to absorb the flavors of the other ingredients in a dish. This Neapolitan classic starts with one of my favorite eggplant preparations: breaded, fried eggplants. The eggplants are parcooked and used as sandwich ends with ham and cheese stuffed in between to create a fried eggplant sandwich reminiscent of a cordon bleu!

These little round sandos can also be made ahead and given a quick reheat in the oven before serving.

MAKES
24 small sandwiches

2 (1-pound) Italian eggplants, peeled and sliced into 48 (¼-inch-thick) rounds

1 pound fresh mozzarella, sliced into 24 very thin slices

12 slices deli ham (½ pound), cut into 2-inch squares

½ cup all-purpose flour

2 large eggs, beaten with 2 tablespoons water

2¼ cups Cheesy Breadcrumbs (see page 267)

1 cup neutral oil, such as canola or grapeseed, for frying

Kosher salt

- Preheat the oven to 350°F.
- Arrange the eggplant slices in a single layer on two baking sheets and roast, rotating the pans halfway through, for 10 to 12 minutes. The eggplant should be limp but not cooked through.
- Place one slice of mozzarella and a few slices of ham on top of an eggplant slice. Top with another eggplant slice to form a sandwich. Repeat until you have 24 sandwiches.
- Set up a breading station: Place the flour, beaten eggs, and breadcrumbs in three separate shallow dishes. Flour each sandwich, shake off the excess, dip in the eggs, and then coat both sides with the breadcrumbs.
- In a large heavy-bottomed skillet, heat the oil over medium-high heat until it reaches 350°F on a candy or deep-fry thermometer. Line a baking sheet with paper towels and set a wire rack on top. Working in batches of 5 or 6, making sure not to overcrowd the pan, fry the sandwiches for about 2 minutes on the first side and 1 minute on the second side, until golden brown.
- Transfer to the rack to drain and immediately sprinkle with salt. Repeat with the remaining sandwiches. Serve hot or at room temperature.

Prosciutto e Melone

alla Fisarmonica

ACCORDION PROSCIUTTO AND MELON

Whenever we travel to Italy in summer, my children have one request, *prosciutto e melone.* Prosciutto di Parma, the gold standard of prosciutto, is produced in Parma, a city in the Emilia-Romagna region. It's made from the hind legs of heritage-bred pigs, and in order to be sold as prosciutto di Parma, it must be inspected by a specialized consortium that designates PDO products in Italy.

Italian melon is incredibly sweet and abundant in the summer months. Paired with the thin-as-paper, salty, fatty prosciutto, it's absolutely the best marriage of flavors. The kids love eating the prosciutto e melone with their hands, but with one complaint: The prosciutto slips off the melon. At home, I found a fun way to serve it, with small pieces of prosciutto and basil leaves tucked into cuts in the melon. Not only is it beautiful, but it's also much easier to eat!

MAKES
8 wedges

1 medium cantaloupe

10 slices prosciutto di Parma, cut into 1-inch pieces

10 to 12 basil leaves

Extra-virgin olive oil

Kosher salt and freshly ground black pepper

◆ Slice the cantaloupe in half crosswise and use a spoon to scoop out all the seeds. Slice each melon half into 4 wedges. Place a sharp knife between the flesh and rind and cut the melon off the rind, stopping a few inches from the end so the flesh is still attached to the rind. Cut very vertical slits into each wedge, stopping about ¼ inch from the bottom of the flesh.

◆ Tuck pieces of prosciutto and basil into the slits, drizzle with oil, and sprinkle with salt and pepper before serving.

CHAPTER 4

CIBO DELLA STRADA

Street Food

Panissa Ligure

POLENTA BITES

In this traditional Ligurian dish, a quick polenta is prepared, firmed up in the fridge, and then cubed and fried. What used to be a quick snack at home has become one of the most beloved street foods in the area. In Italy, the polenta is prepared with a bit of salt, but I decided to mix in a few other ingredients to create an herby, cheesy fried bite. They are great on their own, but a spicy marinara dipping sauce never hurts!

MAKES
64 bites

1 cup quick-cooking polenta (I like Bob's Red Mill)

2 teaspoons kosher salt

1 teaspoon freshly cracked pepper

½ cup mixed fresh herbs (I like oregano, chives, parsley, and basil), chopped

½ cup grated whole-milk mozzarella

Extra-virgin olive oil, for greasing

3 to 4 tablespoons quick-mixing flour, such as Wondra

1 cup neutral oil, such as canola or grapeseed, for frying

½ cup finely grated Parmigiano Reggiano cheese

1 cup Gina's Tomato Sauce (see page 264) or Quick Marinara Sauce (see page 265), for serving (optional)

- In a medium saucepan, bring 3 cups water to a boil. Slowly whisk in the polenta, salt, and pepper. Whisk until the polenta is soft and thickened, about 5 minutes. Turn off the heat and add the herbs and mozzarella. Stir with a wooden spoon to combine.

- Grease an 8-inch square baking dish with olive oil and line it with parchment paper. Spread the polenta in an even layer in the prepared dish. Cover with plastic wrap and refrigerate for 1 hour.

- Remove the polenta from the fridge, peel off the plastic wrap, set a large cutting board over top, and flip the two over so the polenta releases onto the cutting board. Pat the polenta very dry with a paper towel and cut into 1-inch cubes.

- In a medium bowl, combine the polenta cubes and the flour, lightly tossing to coat.

- In a large cast-iron skillet, heat the oil over medium heat until it begins to shimmer. Line a baking sheet with paper towels. Working in batches, shake the excess flour off a handful or two of the polenta cubes and carefully place them in the hot oil, one at a time, in a single layer. Fry for at least 5 minutes, without moving, then flip and cook for 5 minutes more, until browned and crispy on the second side. Transfer the fried polenta to the prepared baking sheet and repeat to fry the remaining polenta. Sprinkle the Parmigiano over the hot polenta bites and serve immediately, with the tomato sauce alongside, if desired.

Fritto Misto *all'Amafitana*

FRIED FISH

Who doesn't love a plate of perfectly fried fresh seafood? Along the Italian coast, you'll see lightly battered fried fish served with lots of fresh lemon. In Palermo or central Naples, you can get a small container of calamari, shrimp, and pieces of white fish served with a toothpick to eat while walking through the city. On the Amalfi Coast, you can stop at one of the restaurants by the water for wine and a dish of the day's catch fried up with lemon and basil. When I spent time there, I couldn't resist this plate of fried delights for aperitivo. Make sure to fry up some lemon to eat with the fish; it's life-changingly good.

SERVES
6 to 8

1 teaspoon garlic powder

1 teaspoon onion powder

1 teaspoon kosher salt, plus more for sprinkling

1 teaspoon freshly ground white pepper

1 cup dry white wine

1 pound calamari, cleaned, bodies cut into 2-inch rings, tentacles detached

1 (½-pound) cod loin, cut into 1¼-inch-thick strips

1 pound extra-large shrimp (26 to 30 per pound), shelled and deveined

6 to 7 cups neutral oil, such as canola or grapeseed, for frying

2 cups self-rising flour

Fried basil leaves, for serving (see Note)

2 lemons: 1 thinly sliced and fried (see Note) and 1 cut into wedges

◆ In a large bowl, combine the garlic powder, onion powder, salt, and white pepper. Add the wine and stir to combine. Add the seafood and toss gently to coat. Cover and marinate in the refrigerator for 1 hour (no longer).

◆ In a medium Dutch oven, heat 2 to 3 inches of the oil over medium-high heat until it reaches 350°F on a candy or deep-fry thermometer. Line a baking sheet with paper towels.

◆ Place the flour in a shallow bowl. Drain the seafood and sort it by type (calamari, cod, and shrimp). Toss each group of seafood in the flour, a few pieces at a time, then transfer to a fine-mesh strainer. Shake the strainer to remove excess flour.

◆ Fry the seafood in the hot oil, one type at a time, until crisp, golden brown, and cooked through, 2 to 3 minutes. Transfer to the prepared baking sheet and sprinkle lightly with salt.

◆ Arrange the fish on a platter and serve with fried basil, fried lemon slices, and lemon wedges for squeezing.

NOTE

To prepare the fried basil leaves and lemon slices, dredge them in self-rising flour. In a small skillet, heat a few glugs of canola or grapeseed oil over medium-high heat until shimmering. Working in batches, if needed, fry the basil and lemon in the hot oil until crisp, 5 to 10 seconds per side. Drain on paper towels.

Fritto Misto Marchigiano

FRIED VEGETABLES

Le Marche is well known for its deep-fried delicacies. Tasty fried bites like Olive all'Ascolana (page 191) are enjoyed with drinks or on the go, while others are sweet treats. Their traditional fritto misto always includes vegetables. The batter works for all kinds of vegetables, but if you find yourself in Le Marche, the vegetables will depend on what is currently coming out of the farm. I love using the batter for thin eggplant, zucchini sticks, canned artichokes, and even green beans.

SERVES
4 to 6

1 teaspoon garlic powder

1 teaspoon onion powder

1 teaspoon kosher salt, plus more as needed

1 teaspoon freshly ground white pepper

2 cups self-rising flour

1 cup unflavored seltzer

1 pound zucchini, cut into 3-inch sticks

½ pound eggplant, cut into 3-inch sticks

1 red bell pepper, seeded and cut into strips

1 (8-ounce) jar marinated artichokes packed in water, drained and patted dry

2 lemons: 1 thinly sliced and 1 cut into wedges

6 to 7 cups neutral oil, such as canola or grapeseed, for frying

- In a large bowl, combine the garlic powder, onion powder, salt, and white pepper. Add the flour and stir to incorporate.

- Slowly pour the seltzer into the flour mixture, whisking to combine. Then add the zucchini, eggplant, bell pepper, artichokes, and sliced lemon to the batter and gently toss to coat.

- In a medium Dutch oven, heat 2 to 3 inches of the oil over medium-high heat until it reaches 350°F on a candy or deep-fry thermometer. Line a baking sheet with paper towels. Fry the vegetables in the hot oil until crisp, golden brown, and cooked through, 2 to 3 minutes. Transfer to the prepared baking sheet to drain and sprinkle lightly with salt.

- Arrange the fritto misto on a platter and serve with the lemon wedges.

UNA
PePeRoncino

Sicilian Cazzilli

POTATO CROQUETTES

If you love mashed potatoes, you will truly adore these croquettes. When walking through the street markets in Palermo, I loved watching them dancing and jumping in the big vats of hot oil. The vendors scoop up the croquettes with huge, slotted ladles, emptying them into cones for on-the-go consumption. Purchased straight from the fryer and devoured with singed fingers, these are the perfect snack to munch on while walking to and from work or school.

I love re-creating this little snack the day after Thanksgiving when I have loads of mashed potatoes left over. If I'm being perfectly honest, I make extra mashed potatoes knowing I can fry these up the next day.

MAKES
eleven 2-ounce croquettes

1½ pounds chilled mashed potatoes

1 tablespoon cornstarch

3 tablespoons finely chopped fresh flat-leaf parsley

2 teaspoons kosher salt, plus more as needed

1 teaspoon freshly ground black pepper

1 cup all-purpose flour

4 cups neutral oil, such as canola or grapeseed, for frying

- Line a baking sheet with parchment paper or a silicone mat.

- In a large bowl, combine the potatoes, cornstarch, parsley, salt, and pepper. Using a 2-ounce ice cream scoop, portion the mixture, one scoop at a time, into balls. Roll the balls between the palms of your hands to form an oval shape. Place the flour in a shallow dish and roll the shaped potato ovals in the flour to coat, setting them on the prepared baking sheet as you work. Refrigerate, uncovered, for 30 minutes.

- In a medium Dutch oven, heat the oil over medium-high heat until it reaches 350°F on a candy or deep-fry thermometer. Line a baking sheet with paper towels. Working in batches, fry the cazzilli for 3 to 4 minutes, until golden brown on all sides. Use a slotted spoon to transfer them to the prepared baking sheet to drain and sprinkle lightly with salt. Serve immediately.

◆

ARANCINI TRIO

Rice Balls, 3 Ways

IN Italy, savory balls of rice, stuffed and fried, can be found throughout the country. What's interesting is that while the basic method is the same, the shape and fillings will vary based on location. Growing up with a Calabrian mother, I was only aware of Calabrian arancini, which are round and made with a "white" rice filling studded with prosciutto, around a melted mozzarella center.

When my family traveled to Italy, I discovered (and enjoyed) *supplì al telefono*, which is the Roman arancini. This version is made with a "red," tomato-based risotto mixed with ground beef and the required mozzarella "moment" in the center. These can be formed into balls or sometimes, small logs.

Recently, I was introduced to *arancine* (with an *e*, as Sicilians have a tendency to add a feminine ending to masculine words). The risotto is flavored with saffron, giving it an orange hue, and then stuffed with a beef-and-pea ragù center. Depending on the chef, they are either round like the Calabrese version or have a cone top.

Here are the three versions. The Calabrian recipe is the most basic and a great place to start. Then you can have fun with the fillings and add tomato sauce (Roma) or saffron (Sicilia) to the rice. For fillings, work your way up from the simple mozzarella cube (Calabria and Roma) to the meat filling (Sicilia).

ARANCINI DI CALABRIA (OPPOSITE CENTER), PAGE 210
SUPPLÌ AL TELEFONO (OPPOSITE RIGHT), PAGE 211
ARANCINE SICILIANA (OPPOSITE LEFT), PAGE 212

Arancini
di Calabria

CALABRIAN RICE BALLS

MAKES
about 21 arancini

2 cups Arborio rice

5 cups chicken broth or water

1 teaspoon kosher salt, plus more as needed

½ tablespoon unsalted butter

1½ teaspoons extra-virgin olive oil

½ cup finely chopped prosciutto

1½ cups Italian-seasoned breadcrumbs (not panko)

1 large egg, beaten

1 teaspoon chopped fresh flat-leaf parsley

⅓ cup finely grated Parmigiano Reggiano cheese, plus more for garnish

4 ounces fresh mozzarella cheese, cut into ¼-inch cubes

4 cups neutral oil, such as canola or grapeseed, for frying

• In a large pot, combine the rice and broth and bring to a boil. Reduce the heat so the liquid simmers, add a pinch of salt, and cover. Cook, stirring occasionally, until the water has been absorbed and the rice is soft and creamy, 15 to 20 minutes.

• Meanwhile, in a small pan, heat the butter and olive oil over medium heat. When the butter has melted, add the prosciutto and cook until it begins to crisp, about 2 minutes. Remove from the heat and set aside.

• Transfer the rice to a large baking sheet, spread it out in an even layer, and let cool for 10 minutes. (The rice can be cooled and stored in an airtight container in the refrigerator overnight.)

• While the rice is cooling, pour ½ cup water into a shallow bowl. Place the breadcrumbs in a separate shallow bowl. Set both aside.

• Transfer the cooled rice to a large bowl and stir in the prosciutto, egg, parsley, Parmigiano, and salt. Keep the baking sheet at hand.

• Using a 2-ounce ice cream scoop or a ⅓-cup measuring cup and lightly wetted hands, form a 2-inch ball with the rice mixture. Make an indentation in the middle and add a cube of mozzarella. Enclose the cheese in the rice and reshape into a ball. Set on the baking sheet and repeat with the remaining rice mixture.

• Using your hands, lightly moisten each rice ball with water, then roll in the breadcrumbs. Return them to the baking sheet.

• In a medium Dutch oven, heat the neutral oil over medium-high heat until it reaches 350°F on a candy or deep-fry thermometer. Line a baking sheet with paper towels. Carefully drop 4 rice balls into the oil (they should fully submerge) and cook until the outsides are golden brown, about 3 minutes. If your pot is wide enough, carefully roll the rice balls in the oil to ensure even cooking on all sides. Transfer to the prepared baking sheet to drain. Season with salt. Repeat with the remaining rice balls.

• The arancini are best eaten at room temperature, sprinkled with Parmigiano.

Supplì
al Telefono

ROMAN RICE BALLS

MAKES
about 21 arancini

2 cups Arborio rice

4 to 5 cups beef broth or water

½ tablespoon unsalted butter

1½ teaspoons extra-virgin olive oil

1 pound 90% lean ground beef

2 teaspoons kosher salt, plus more as needed

1 cup canned tomato sauce

⅓ cup grated Parmigiano Reggiano, plus more for garnish

1½ cups Cheesy Breadcrumbs (see page 267) or store-bought Italian seasoned breadcrumbs (not panko)

4 ounces fresh mozzarella cheese, cut into ¼-inch cubes

4 cups neutral oil, such as canola or grapeseed, for frying

• In a large pot, combine the rice and broth and bring to a boil. Reduce the heat so liquid simmers, add a pinch of salt, and cover. Cook, stirring occasionally, until the water is absorbed and the rice is soft and creamy, 15 to 20 minutes.

• Meanwhile, in a small pan, heat the butter and olive oil over medium heat. When the butter is melted, add the beef and salt. Cook until the beef is no longer pink, 6 to 7 minutes. Drain the fat from the pan, add the tomato sauce and Parmigiano, and stir to combine. Remove from the heat and set aside.

• Scoop the rice into the beef sauce and stir to combine. Taste and season with more salt, if needed. Transfer the mixture to a baking sheet, spread it out in an even layer, and let cool for 20 minutes, then cover with plastic wrap and refrigerate for 20 minutes more. (The rice can be cooled and stored in an airtight container in the refrigerator overnight.)

• While the rice is cooling, pour ½ cup water into a shallow bowl. Place the breadcrumbs in a separate shallow bowl. Set both aside.

• Line a baking sheet with parchment paper or a silicone mat. Using a 2-ounce ice cream scoop or a ⅓-cup measuring cup and lightly wetted hands, form a 2-inch ball with the rice mixture. Make an indentation in the middle and add a cube or two of mozzarella. Enclose the cheese in the rice and reshape into a ball. Set it on the prepared baking sheet and repeat with the remaining rice mixture.

• Using your hands, lightly moisten each rice ball with water, then roll in the breadcrumbs. Return them to the baking sheet.

• In a medium Dutch oven, heat the neutral oil over medium-high heat until it reaches 350°F on a candy or deep-fry thermometer. Line a baking sheet with paper towels. Carefully drop 4 rice balls into the oil (they should fully submerge) and cook until the outside is golden brown, about 3 minutes. If your pot is wide enough, carefully roll the rice balls in the oil to ensure even cooking on all sides. Transfer to the prepared baking sheet to drain. Season with salt. Repeat with the remaining rice balls. The arancini are best eaten at room temperature, sprinkled with Parmigiano.

Arancine *Siciliana*

SICILIAN RICE BALLS

MAKES
15 arancine

2 cups Arborio rice

5 cups chicken broth or water

Kosher salt

½ teaspoon ground saffron

½ tablespoon unsalted butter

1½ teaspoons extra-virgin olive oil

½ cup finely chopped yellow onion

½ pound 90% lean ground beef

1½ teaspoons tomato paste

½ cup red wine

1 cup canned tomato sauce

½ cup canned small peas, drained

1½ cups Cheesy Breadcrumbs (see page 267) or store-bought Italian-seasoned breadcrumbs (not panko)

1 large egg, beaten

⅓ cup finely grated Parmigiano Reggiano cheese, plus more for garnish

4 cups neutral oil, such as canola or grapeseed, for frying

• In a large pot, combine the rice and broth and bring to a boil. Reduce the heat so the liquid simmers, add a pinch of salt, and cover. Cook, stirring occasionally, until the water has been absorbed and the rice is soft and creamy, 15 to 20 minutes.

• Meanwhile, in a small pan, heat the butter and olive oil over medium heat. When the butter has melted, add the onion and cook until it begins to soften, about 3 minutes. Add the beef, breaking it up with a wooden spoon, and cook until it is no longer pink, 6 to 7 minutes. Season with salt, add the tomato paste, and stir to incorporate.

• Raise the heat to high and add the red wine. Cook, stirring frequently, until the wine reduces a bit, about 3 minutes. Add the tomato sauce and peas and fold them into the meat. Reduce the heat to low, season with salt, and simmer until the ragù is thickened, about 15 minutes. Remove from the heat and set aside to cool.

• When the rice is cooked, transfer it to a large baking sheet, spread it into an even layer, and let cool for 10 minutes. (The rice can be cooled and stored in an airtight container in the refrigerator overnight.)

• While the rice is cooling, pour ½ cup water into a shallow bowl. Place the breadcrumbs in a separate shallow bowl. Set both aside.

• Transfer the rice to a large bowl and add the egg, Parmigiano, and 1 teaspoon salt. Stir to combine.

• Line a baking sheet with parchment paper or a silicone mat. Using a 2-ounce ice cream scoop or a ⅓-cup measuring cup and lightly wetted hands, form a 2-inch ball with the rice mixture. Make an indentation in the middle and add a tablespoon of the ragù. Enclose the ragù in the rice and reshape into a ball, then set on the prepared baking sheet. Repeat with the remaining rice mixture.

• Using your hands, lightly moisten each rice ball with water, then roll in the breadcrumbs. Return them to the baking sheet.

• In a medium Dutch oven, heat the neutral oil over medium-high heat until it reaches 350°F on a candy or deep-fry thermometer. Line a baking sheet with paper towels. Carefully drop 4 rice balls into the oil (they should fully submerge) and cook until the outside is golden brown, about 3 minutes. If your pot is wide enough, carefully roll the rice balls in the oil to ensure even cooking on all sides. Transfer to the prepared baking sheet to drain. Season with salt. Repeat with the remaining rice balls.

• The arancine are best eaten at room temperature, sprinkled with Parmigiano.

Frittatina di Pasta

FRIED PASTA

This Neapolitan snack is made from leftover pasta. Cold pasta is mixed with sauce, either tomato sauce or a thick béchamel, some eggs, and melty grated cheese. At home, most fry it up in a pan and serve it in slices. On the streets, it is pressed and cut into squares, enrobed in a bread crust, and deep-fried. This recipe, which also includes peas and ham, is inspired by the fried squares I had at a small street stand.

MAKES
24 squares

1 pound elbow pasta

4 cups whole milk

1 tablespoon extra-virgin olive oil

4 tablespoons (57 grams) unsalted butter

2¼ cups all-purpose flour

16 ounces grated mozzarella cheese (about 4 cups)

8 ounces grated Parmigiano Reggiano cheese (about 2 cups)

1 cup (5 ounces) frozen peas, rinsed

1 pound deli ham, cut into 1-inch squares

2 teaspoons kosher salt, plus more as needed

4 large eggs

2½ cups Cheesy Breadcrumbs (see page 267) or store-bought Italian-seasoned breadcrumbs (not panko)

4 cups neutral oil, such as canola or grapeseed, for frying

◆ Bring a medium pot of salted water to a boil and cook the pasta according to package directions. In a separate pot, heat the milk on low. Drain the pasta, transfer it to a large bowl, and stir in the olive oil. Set aside.

◆ Using the same pot the pasta was cooked in, melt the butter over medium heat. Add ¼ cup of the flour and whisk until golden brown, about 2 to 3 minutes. Slowly pour the warm milk into the roux and whisk continuously until well combined and the mixture coats the back of a spoon, about 8 minutes. Remove from heat. Stir in the mozzarella and Parmigiano. Add the pasta, peas, ham, and salt and stir to fully coat the pasta.

◆ Line the bottom and sides of a deep 9 × 13-inch baking dish with plastic wrap. Pour the pasta mixture into the dish and let cool completely. Cover the pasta with plastic wrap, pressing it onto the pasta. Refrigerate overnight.

RECIPE CONTINUES

GIRARROSTO FIORENZANO
GIRARROSTO
FIORENZANO
POLLO allo SPIEDO-PIZZE FRITTE-FRITTURA all 'ITALIANA-FRITTURA d
FIORENZANO
dal 1897

- Remove the plastic wrap and place a large cutting board on top of the pasta. Holding the dish and cutting board together, invert the pasta onto the board and cut it into 24 pieces.

- Set up a dredging station: Line a baking sheet with parchment paper. In a shallow bowl, beat the eggs. In two other shallow bowls, place the breadcrumbs in one and the remaining 2 cups flour in the other.

- Coat a pasta square with flour, shaking off the excess. Dip it into the egg and allow the excess to drip off, then coat the square in breadcrumbs. Place it on the prepared baking sheet and repeat with the remaining squares.

- In a medium Dutch oven, heat the neutral oil over medium-high heat until it reaches 350°F on a candy or deep-fry thermometer. Line a baking sheet with paper towels. Fry 3 or 4 squares at a time until golden brown and warm on the inside, 2 minutes per side. Transfer to the prepared baking sheet to drain, sprinkle with salt, if desired, and serve immediately.

VARIATION

You can also make these in the air fryer: Spray the pasta squares with olive oil spray on all sides. Preheat the air fryer to 400°F. Cook for 8 minutes, flipping halfway through. Sprinkle with salt.

Spiedini di Carne

STUFFED MEAT SKEWERS

In Palermo, these stuffed meat pockets are threaded onto skewers and grilled day and night and sold by the thousands to hungry pedestrians. Traditionally, they are made with thin veal cutlets, but chicken works just as well for those who don't eat veal. Like they do in Palermo, you can make them early in the morning and pop them in the oven when you are ready to eat.

MAKES
6 skewers

¾ cup breadcrumbs

¼ cup freshly grated Parmigiano Reggiano cheese

1¼ teaspoons kosher salt, plus more as needed

¼ cup tomato sauce

3 to 4 tablespoons extra-virgin olive oil

1½ pounds veal or chicken cutlets (about 8)

5 or 6 slices deli ham

25 to 30 (¼- to ½-inch) cubes provolone or caciocavallo cheese (about 2 ounces)

½ red onion, cut into 2-inch pieces

20 to 25 dried bay leaves

Freshly ground black pepper

1 teaspoon dried oregano

Lemon wedges, for serving

SPECIAL EQUIPMENT

6 wooden skewers

- Soak 6 wooden skewers in water for 1 hour. Preheat the oven to 350°F.
- In a medium bowl, combine ½ cup of the breadcrumbs, the Parmigiano, ¼ teaspoon of the salt, the tomato sauce, and 1 tablespoon of the oil and stir. Set aside.
- On a cutting board, pound the cutlets very thin with a meat mallet. Place a strip of ham on top of each cutlet, then cut them into strips that are 2 inches wide and 3 inches long. Sprinkle each strip with1 teaspoon of the breadcrumb mixture and place 1 cube of provolone on top.
- Roll up the cutlets around the filling, tucking in the sides as you roll so the filling does not come out during cooking.
- Thread a soaked skewer in this order: onion, meat roll, and bay leaf until the skewer is three quarters full. Repeat with the remaining skewers and ingredients.
- Drizzle skewers on all sides with a tablespoon or so of oil, then season them on all sides with salt, pepper, oregano, and the remaining breadcrumbs.
- Brush a baking sheet with a few tablespoons of oil and arrange the breaded skewers on top.
- Bake for 30 minutes, until the meat is cooked through. Turn on the broiler and broil for 2 minutes to char the onions and brown the breadcrumbs.
- Immediately squeeze the lemon wedges over the skewers and serve immediately.

Mangia e Beve

"EAT AND DRINK"
(BACON-WRAPPED SPRING ONIONS)

The name of these made me laugh when I heard it, as the title is the instruction. Served with ice-cold Italian beer, these salty snacks use onions as an edible skewer. In Italy, the meat is a fresh, thinly sliced pancetta, which is similar to American bacon. If you can't find spring onions, scallions are the perfect substitute.

MAKES
12 "skewers"

12 spring onions

12 thin-cut slices bacon

Lemon wedges, for serving

- Preheat the oven to 450°F.
- Remove the outermost leaves from the onions and slice off the bottoms and very tops. Wrap each onion in a slice of bacon from tip to end. Arrange them in a row on a baking sheet.
- Bake for 10 minutes. Remove and carefully flip the onions, then bake until the onions are soft and the bacon is crisp, 15 to 20 minutes more.
- Squeeze the lemon wedges over the skewers and serve immediately.

Pampanella

PAPRIKA RIBS

Pampanella is Molise's best-known street food. Various cuts of pork are slow cooked with lots of paprika and spice and finished with vinegar. Famous for its deep red color, it's the perfect party food. The Molisani serve it with hunks of bread to help take down the heat and acid. For this version, I used baby back ribs, as the preparation reminds me of how ribs are prepared in Memphis: lots of spice with a vinegar finish.

MAKES
1 rack of ribs

1 ($2\frac{1}{2}$-pound) rack baby back pork ribs, membrane removed

2 teaspoons kosher salt

2 teaspoons garlic powder

2 teaspoons smoked paprika

2 teaspoons sweet paprika

2 teaspoons chili powder

3 tablespoons red wine vinegar, plus more if needed

- Place a large piece of aluminum foil on a baking sheet. Place a piece of parchment paper, just a bit smaller than the foil, over the foil. Place the rack of ribs on top of the parchment.

- In a small bowl, combine the salt, garlic powder, both paprikas, and chili powder. Rub the mixture into the meat, evenly covering all the ribs on both sides.

- Refrigerate the ribs, covered loosely with plastic wrap, for at least 1 hour or up to overnight.

- Preheat the oven to 275°F. Wrap the ribs in the parchment paper, then pull up the foil on all sides and seal it closed over the parchment. Bake for 2 hours.

- Remove the ribs from the oven and carefully unwrap them. Baste the ribs with the vinegar. (If the ribs seem dry, add a few more tablespoons of vinegar.)

- Turn on the broiler and broil the ribs for 3 minutes, until browned and charred in spots.

- Cut the meat between the ribs and serve.

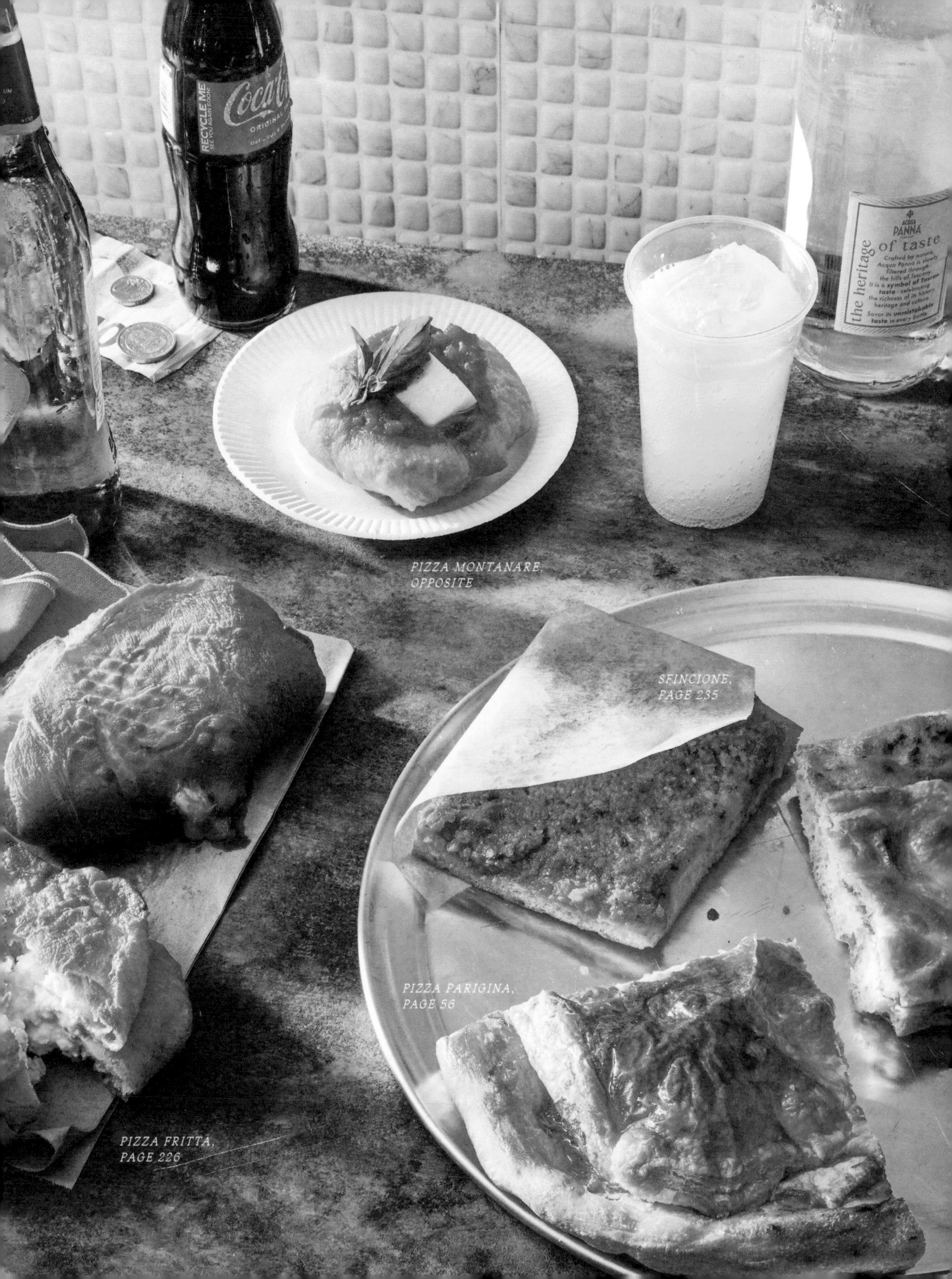
Coca-Cola
RECYCLE ME
ACQUA PANNA
the heritage of taste
PIZZA MONTANARE, OPPOSITE
SFINCIONE, PAGE 235
PIZZA PARIGINA, PAGE 56
PIZZA FRITTA, PAGE 226

Pizza Montanare

FRIED PIZZA

Fried pizza is a snack many of us have had at church fairs and carnivals. Unfortunately, here in the States, it is often overdusted with confectioners' sugar or served with sauce and a bit of grated mystery cheese from that awful green can. Can we even call that Parmigiano? Anyway, in Naples this preparation is called *montanare*. After the dough fries, a dollop of sauce and a bit of fresh mozzarella or grated Parmigiano cover the top, which is crowned with a basil leaf.

MAKES
10 small pizzettes

½ recipe All-Purpose Pizza Dough (see page 263)

½ cup neutral oil, such as canola or grapeseed, for frying

1 cup Gina's Tomato Sauce (see page 264) or Quick Marinara Sauce (see page 265), or 1 cup canned tomato sauce

1 pound fresh mozzarella cheese, cut into small cubes

10 small basil leaves

- Portion the dough into ten 3- to 4-ounce pieces. Reroll the pieces into balls, using a dusting of flour if needed. Place the dough balls on a baking sheet and cover with a kitchen towel while you prepare the oil.

- Preheat the oven to 350°F.

- In a cast-iron skillet, heat the oil over medium heat until it reaches 350°F on a candy or deep-fry thermometer. Line a baking sheet with parchment paper.

- Place the dough balls on a lightly floured work surface and press them into flat 5-inch disks.

- Place two disks into the oil and fry for 3 minutes, then flip and fry for 3 minutes more. Poke any bubbles that form with a fork to maintain a flat surface.

- Transfer to the prepared baking sheet. Spoon 1 tablespoon sauce in the middle of each pizzette and sprinkle with ¼ cup mozzarella.

- Bake for 5 minutes, until the cheese is melted. Garnish each pizzette with a basil leaf and serve immediately.

Pizza Fritta

FRIED CALZONE

In Italy, a fried pizza is also called *pizza fritta*, but in Naples pizza fritta is actually a fried calzone. Each *pizzaiolo* gets creative with fillings, but cheese and meat are the standard. If you don't want to fry pork, diced salami or boiled ham can be substituted—they are also traditional and just as delicious.

MAKES
8 calzones

2 cups whole-milk ricotta

2 teaspoons kosher salt

1 recipe All-Purpose Pizza Dough (see page 263)

All-purpose flour, for dusting

1 tablespoon extra-virgin olive oil

½ pound ground pork

1 teaspoon freshly ground black pepper

1 cup shredded low-moisture mozzarella cheese

2 quarts neutral oil, such as canola or grapeseed, for frying

- In a small bowl, combine the ricotta and 1 teaspoon of the salt. Set aside.

- Portion the dough into eight 3- to 4-ounce pieces. Reroll the pieces into balls, using a dusting of flour if needed. Place the dough balls on a baking sheet. Cover with a kitchen towel while you fry the pork.

- Line a plate with a paper towel. In a large skillet, heat the oil over medium heat until shimmering, about 2 minutes. Add the pork and cook, breaking it up with a wooden spoon, until no longer pink, 6 to 7 minutes. Season with the remaining 1 teaspoon salt and the pepper and stir to combine. Use a slotted spoon to transfer the pork to the prepared plate to drain.

- Place the dough balls on a lightly floured work surface and press them into flat 5-inch disks. Spoon a scant ¼ cup of ricotta onto one half of each of the disks, followed by a tablespoon of pork and a sprinkle of mozzarella. Use a floured fork to fold the other side of the disk over the filling and press down along the edge to seal the calzone.

- In a large Dutch oven, heat the neutral oil over medium-high heat until it reaches 350°F on a candy or deep-fry thermometer. Line a baking sheet with paper towels.

- Place 2 calzones into the oil and fry for 3 minutes, flip, and fry for 3 minutes more. Use a slotted spoon to transfer the calzone to the prepared baking sheet to drain. Serve immediately.

Pizza Margherita

CLASSIC MARGHERITA PIZZA

The Margherita is the Italian classic pizza, colored red, white, and green. A smear of sauce, torn, fresh mozzarella dotted along the top, a scatter of fresh basil, and olive oil drizzled right as the pizza is pulled from the oven—this pizza is the gold standard of Neapolitan pizzerias. Start with this combination, then use the dough as a blank canvas for whatever you like.

MAKES
one 10-inch pizza

3 to 4 tablespoons extra-virgin olive oil, plus more for finishing

½ recipe All-Purpose Pizza Dough (see page 263)

½ cup Gina's Tomato Sauce (see page 264) or Quick Marinara Sauce (see page 265)

5 ounces fresh mozzarella cheese, torn into pieces

4 basil leaves

- Position a rack in the center of the oven and preheat the oven to 500°F.
- Brush a baking sheet with 3 to 4 tablespoons of the oil.
- Carefully press the dough into the prepared baking sheet to create a large 10-inch circle. Using your fingers, press an indentation around the edge, about ½ inch in, to create a crust line, leaving the center of the dough a bit puffed.
- Spread the tomato sauce in a thin layer just to the indentation line, leaving a ½-inch border.
- Scatter the mozzarella evenly over the sauce. Drizzle more oil all over the crust.
- Bake for 10 minutes. If the edges are not charred to your liking, move the pizza to the top rack, turn on the broiler, and broil for 2 to 5 minutes.
- Top with the basil and drizzle with oil. Slice and serve immediately.

Pizza Marinara

MARINARA PIZZA

A marinara pizza is super simple but still very delicious. There is no cheese on this pizza. Instead, the crust is baked with lots of extra-virgin olive oil and tomato sauce. It's light and a great addition to any pizza party. I love serving it with a big salad. For this pizza, you will be using your fingers to create indentations all over the dough, leaving a ½ inch border. These indentations will hold the garlic oil.

MAKES
one 10-inch pizza

½ cup extra-virgin olive oil, plus more as needed

2 garlic cloves, minced

1 teaspoon kosher salt

½ recipe All-Purpose Pizza Dough (see page 263)

1 cup Gina's Tomato Sauce (see page 264) or Quick Marinara Sauce (see page 265)

1 teaspoon crushed red pepper flakes (optional)

- Position a rack in the center of the oven and preheat the oven to 500°F. Brush a baking sheet with a tablespoon or so of the oil.

- In a small skillet, heat ½ cup of the oil over low heat. Add the garlic and salt and cook until the garlic begins to sizzle and brown, about 2 minutes. Remove from the heat and set aside to cool for 5 minutes.

- Carefully press the dough into the prepared baking sheet to create a large 10-inch circle. Using your fingers, make indentations all over the dough and create a ½-inch border around the edge.

- Drizzle the garlic oil over the dough and spread evenly so that the oil catches in the small pockets in the dough. Spread the tomato sauce over the garlic oil and sprinkle the red pepper flakes over top (if using).

- Bake for 10 minutes. If the edges are not charred to your liking, move the pizza to the top rack, turn on the broiler, and broil for 2 to 5 minutes.

- Drizzle the pizza with oil, slice, and serve immediately.

Neapolitan Panini

NEAPOLITAN PIZZA SANDWICHES

In Naples, this on-the-go street panino traditionally is stuffed with various salamis, chopped hard-boiled eggs, and cheese and then baked. Initially created to use up leftover pizza dough, it became a street food mainstay, as it is so easy to eat and the filling options are endless. Treat the fillings as you would toppings for pizza: Choose your favorites.

MAKES
6 panini

4 large eggs

4 ounces pancetta, chopped into ¼-inch dice

1 recipe All-Purpose Pizza Dough (see page 263)

2 cups shredded low-moisture mozzarella cheese

½ cup 1-inch cubes fresh mozzarella cheese

4 ounces chopped salami

1 cup finely grated Parmigiano Reggiano cheese

Kosher salt

- Place 3 of the eggs in a saucepan and fill with enough cold water to cover. Bring to a boil, turn off the heat, and cover the pan. Set aside for 10 minutes. Drain, let cool for 5 minutes, and peel. Chop the eggs into small dice. Set aside.

- Line a plate with a paper towel. In a small saucepan, cook the pancetta over medium-low heat until crisp, 5 to 6 minutes. Use a slotted spoon to transfer the pancetta to the prepared plate.

- On a lightly floured work surface, roll the dough into a large rectangle, approximately 12 × 22 inches.

- Top the dough with an even layer of the shredded and cubed mozzarellas, eggs, pancetta, and salami. Starting at one of the shorter edges, carefully roll the dough to create a log.

- Line a baking sheet with parchment paper. In a small bowl, beat the remaining egg with 1 tablespoon water.

- Cut the log into six 3-inch panini; they should look similar to a stromboli. Place on the prepared baking sheet and brush with the egg wash. Sprinkle a pinch of salt over each panini, cover with a kitchen towel, and set aside in warm spot to rest for 1 hour.

- Preheat the oven to 400°F.

- Bake for 25 for 35 minutes, until the dough is cooked and slightly browned on the top. Serve warm or at room temperature.

Girelle

"SWIRLED" PANINI

Girelle means "swirl" in Italian. Here the panini is baked cut-side up to create a swirled bun.

MAKES
8 girelle

1 tablespoon extra-virgin olive oil

1 pound sweet Italian sausage, casings removed

1 recipe All-Purpose Dough (see page 263)

8 ounces mascarpone cheese, at room temperature

3 cups shredded low-moisture mozzarella cheese

10 ounces frozen spinach, thawed and squeezed of excess water

1 large egg, beaten with 1 tablespoon water, for egg wash

Kosher salt

◆ Line a plate with a paper towel. In a large skillet, heat the oil over medium-high heat. Add the sausage and use a wooden spoon to break it into pieces. Cook, stirring frequently, until the sausage is golden brown and cooked through, 7 to 9 minutes. Use a slotted spoon to transfer the sausage to the prepared plate. Set aside to cool to room temperature.

◆ Meanwhile, preheat the oven to 375°F. Line two baking sheets with parchment paper. On a lightly floured work surface, roll the dough into a large rectangle, about 12 × 22 inches.

◆ Spread the mascarpone cheese evenly over the dough. Sprinkle the mozzarella evenly over the mascarpone, followed by the spinach. Spoon the sausage over top in an even layer.

◆ Starting at one of the shorter edges, carefully roll the dough to create a log.

◆ Cut the log into eight 1½-inch-wide slices. Carefully lay the slices onto the prepared baking sheets cut-side up and brush with the egg wash. Sprinkle a pinch of salt over each pinwheel. Cover with a kitchen towel and let rest in a warm place while the oven preheats.

◆ Bake for 25 to 30 minutes, until the dough is cooked and slightly browned on the top. Serve warm or at room temperature.

Quattro Stagioni

THE FOUR SEASONS

Artichokes represent spring, tomatoes or basil represent summer, mushrooms represent autumn, and the ham or prosciutto and olives represent winter in this "four seasons" pizza. Another variation is the *quattro formaggi*: Swap out the vegetables and meat for 2 ounces each shredded low-moisture mozzarella, Fontina, Asiago, and Pecorino Romano cheeses.

MAKES
one 10-inch pizza

3 to 4 tablespoons extra-virgin olive oil, plus more for finishing

½ recipe All-Purpose Pizza Dough (see page 263)

½ cup Gina's Tomato Sauce (see page 264) or Quick Marinara Sauce (see page 265)

5 ounces fresh mozzarella cheese, torn into pieces

4 or 5 jarred marinated artichoke hearts, drained and quartered

4 mushrooms (any variety), thinly sliced

3 slices deli boiled ham, chopped

2 small Campari tomatoes, quartered and seeded, or ½ cup pitted olives

3 basil leaves, torn

◆ Position a rack in the center of the oven and preheat the oven to 500°F. Brush a baking sheet with 3 to 4 tablespoons of the oil.

◆ Carefully press the dough into the prepared baking sheet to create a large 10-inch circle. Using your fingers, press an indentation around the edge, about ½ inch in, to create a crust line, leaving the center of the dough a bit puffed.

◆ Spread the tomato sauce in a thin layer just to the indentation line, leaving a ½-inch border. Scatter the mozzarella evenly over the sauce. Lay the artichoke hearts over one-quarter of the pizza, the mushrooms over another quarter, the ham over another quarter, and the tomatoes over the last quarter. Lay the torn basil over the tomatoes.

◆ Bake for 10 minutes. If the edges are not charred to your liking, move the pizza to the top rack, turn on the broiler, and broil for 2 to 5 minutes. Drizzle with oil, slice, and serve immediately.

Panzerotti

PUGLIESE FRIED CALZONE

In Puglia, *pizza fritta* is called *panzerotti* and is filled with tomato sauce and mozzarella.

MAKES
8 calzones

1 cup Gina's Tomato Sauce (see page 264) or Quick Marinara Sauce (see page 265)

1 recipe All-Purpose Pizza Dough (page 263)

2 1/2 cups shredded low-moisture mozzarella cheese

2 quarts neutral oil, such as canola or grapeseed, for frying

All-purpose flour, for dusting

• Line a mesh sieve with paper towels and set it over a medium bowl. Pour the tomato sauce into the prepared sieve and set it aside to drain for 10 minutes. (The tomato sauce will be slightly thicker as a result.)

• Portion the dough into eight 3- to 4-ounce pieces. Reroll the pieces into balls, using a dusting of flour if needed. Place the dough balls on a baking sheet.

• Place the dough balls on a lightly floured work surface and press them into flat 5-inch disks. Spoon 1 tablespoon of the tomato sauce over one half of each disk, followed by 3 tablespoons of the mozzarella cheese. Use a floured fork to fold the other side of the disk over the filling and press down along the edge to seal the calzone.

• In a large Dutch oven, heat the neutral oil over medium-high heat until it reaches 350°F on a candy or deep-fry thermometer. Line a baking sheet with paper towels. Place 2 calzones into the oil and fry for 3 minutes, then flip and fry for 3 minutes more. Use a slotted spoon to transfer the calzones to the prepared baking sheet to drain. Serve immediately.

Sfincione

SICILIAN SHEET PAN PIZZA

The markets of Palermo are a wonderment of sight, sound, and delicious smells. Street vendors shouting, people lined up for an inexpensive yet incredibly filling and delicious midmorning snack. Fish, spices, jars of condiments and cookies for sale, and many fried snacks or baking delicacies lined up as far as the eye can see.

One of the most famous treats is *sfincione*. Sfincione is to Palermo what pizza is to Naples. A supple, focaccia-like dough piled with an oniony sauce and crunchy breadcrumb topping. Hidden between the sauce and dough is a layer of cheese. Yes, the pizza toppings are reversed, but it still works. Sfincione can be found in bakeries, pizzerias, and *rosticcerie* and is even sold hot in supermarkets. This snack is eaten in the morning, at noon, or as a treat on the way home from work.

MAKES
16 pan pizzas

DOUGH

3¾ cups warm water (110°F)

1 (¼-ounce) packet active dry yeast (2¼ teaspoons)

2 teaspoons sugar

5 cups (600 grams) bread flour, plus more for dusting

1 tablespoon kosher salt

2 tablespoons extra-virgin olive oil

SAUCE

2 tablespoons extra-virgin olive oil

1 to 2 teaspoons crushed red pepper flakes

4 anchovy fillets (optional)

1 teaspoon kosher salt

3 medium onions, thinly sliced (3 cups)

1 tablespoon tomato paste

3 cups Gina's Tomato Sauce (see page 264) or Quick Marinara Sauce (see page 265)

TO ASSEMBLE

¼ cup extra-virgin olive oil, plus more for drizzling

12 thin slices deli provolone or mozzarella cheese (about ½ pound)

¼ cup Cheesy Breadcrumbs (see page 267)

RECIPE CONTINUES

• MAKE THE DOUGH: In a small bowl, whisk together 1¼ cups of the water, the yeast, and the sugar. Let stand for 5 minutes.

• In the bowl of a stand mixer fitted with the dough hook, combine the flour and salt.

• With the mixer running, add the remaining 2½ cups water and mix until a shaggy dough forms, about 2 minutes. Add the yeast mixture and mix for 1 minute more. Do not overmix; the dough will be very wet.

• Transfer the dough to a lightly floured work surface. Use a bench scraper to scoop out any dough sticking to the bowl.

• Carefully fold the dough into a messy ball that can be picked up.

• Drizzle the oil into a large bowl and swirl to coat. Place the dough into the bowl, cover with a kitchen towel, and set it in a warm spot to rise for 2 hours, until doubled in size. While the dough is rising, make the sauce.

• MEANWHILE, MAKE THE SAUCE: In a large skillet, heat the oil over medium heat until shimmering, about 2 minutes. Add the red pepper flakes and anchovy fillets (if using) and move them around the pan until they dissolve. Add the salt and onions and stir to coat in the oil.

• Cook the onions, stirring occasionally to encourage even cooking, until translucent and browning at the edges, 8 to 9 minutes. Add the tomato paste and stir to incorporate. Add the tomato sauce and raise the heat to medium-high.

• When the tomato sauce begins to boil, reduce the heat to low and simmer, partially covered, for 20 minutes. Remove from heat and set aside to cool to room temperature.

• Pour the ¼ cup olive oil onto a 13 × 18-inch baking sheet and set the dough on top. Press into the dough with all ten fingers, stretching it toward the edges of the pan. When it begins to resist, loosely cover it with plastic wrap and a kitchen towel. Set it in a warm spot to proof for 15 minutes.

• Position the oven racks in the middle and upper third of the oven and preheat the oven to 425°F.

• Press into the proofed dough with your fingertips. The dough will easily move to the edges of the pan.

• Arrange the cheese evenly over the dough. Spoon the sauce over the cheese and spread it evenly to the edges. Sprinkle the breadcrumbs over the sauce, evenly and to the edges.

• Drizzle the pizza with oil. Bake for 10 minutes on the middle rack, then rotate the pan and place it on the top rack and bake for 10 to 15 minutes more. The bottom of the pizza should be golden brown and the breadcrumbs should be toasted. Serve immediately or at room temperature.

◆

BRIOCHE, DOLCE E SALATA

Brioche, Sweet and Savory

IN Sicily, brioche is the bread of the streets. One dough is used in many street food recipes and creates several delicious snacks eaten in and around Palermo. A *rosticceria* is a bakery/deli where fried and baked snacks, both sweet (*dolce*) and savory (*salato*), are made daily. Vendors serve them on a little tray wrapped in squares of parchment; these treats are eaten throughout the day and are the quintessential street food.

When I traveled through Sicily, I was amazed at how one dough could create so many unique creations based on whether it was baked or fried and whether stuffed with meats, sauces, and cheese or pastry creams, sweet cheeses, chocolate, and gelato! Master this dough, both the savory and sweet versions, and the possibilities for ultimate snacking are endless.

Brioche Dolce

SWEET BRIOCHE DOUGH

MAKES
enough for
12 pastries or one
11-inch round loaf

¾ cup (171 grams) warm whole milk (110°F)

½ cup (100 grams) plus ¼ teaspoon sugar

1 (¼-ounce) packet active dry yeast (2¼ teaspoons)

1¾ cups (203 grams) 00 flour, plus more for dusting

1 cup (120 grams) bread flour

2 large eggs, at room temperature, beaten

Zest of 1 lemon

1 teaspoon kosher salt

5 tablespoons unsalted butter, at room temperature

4 cups neutral oil, such as canola or grapeseed, for frying

- In a small bowl, whisk together the milk, ¼ teaspoon of the sugar, and the yeast. Let stand for 5 minutes.

- In the bowl of a stand mixer fitted with the dough hook, combine both flours, the remaining ½ cup sugar, the eggs, lemon zest, and salt. With the mixer on medium-low, add the milk mixture and beat until just combined. The dough will be tacky, but do not add more flour at this point.

- With the mixer running, slowly drop pieces of the butter into the dough, kneading them in until the butter dissolves into the dough before adding a few more pieces; when you've added all the butter, the dough should be soft and supple. Add more flour, a few tablespoons at a time, if the dough begins to stick to the sides of the bowl. The dough will be very soft but should also be smooth. This should take 3 to 5 minutes.

- Scrape down the sides of the bowl and form the dough into a ball. Cover it with a kitchen towel and set in a warm spot to rise for 2 hours.

Brioche Salato

SAVORY BRIOCHE DOUGH

MAKES
enough for
12 pastries or one
11-inch round loaf

1¼ cups (285 grams) warm whole milk (110°F)

2 tablespoons sugar

1 (¼-ounce) packet active dry yeast (2¼ teaspoons)

4 cups (480 grams) all-purpose flour

½ cup (50 grams) finely grated Parmigiano Reggiano cheese

2 large eggs, at room temperature, beaten

1 teaspoon kosher salt

5 tablespoons unsalted butter, cut into small pieces, at room temperature

- In a small bowl, whisk together the milk, sugar, and yeast. Let stand for 5 minutes.

- In the bowl of a stand mixer fitted with the dough hook, combine the flour, Parmigiano, eggs, and salt. With the mixer on medium-low, add the milk mixture and beat until just combined. The dough will be tacky, but do not add more flour at this point.

- With the mixer running, slowly drop pieces of the butter into the dough, kneading them in until the butter dissolves into the dough before adding a few more pieces; when you've added all the butter, the dough should be soft and supple. Add more flour, a few tablespoons at a time, if the dough begins to stick to the sides of the bowl. The dough will be very soft but should also be smooth. This should take 3 to 5 minutes.

- Scrape down the sides of the bowl and form the dough into a ball. Cover it with a kitchen towel and set in a warm spot to rise for 2 hours.

The Iris

FRIED CANNOLI CREAM DOUGHNUT

This fried brioche doughnut is filled with ricotta cream and chocolate chips. What I loved about this doughnut is, prior to frying, the dough is enrobed in breadcrumbs, giving the exterior a crunchy, sandy texture. The filling is, quite simply, a cannoli cream. It tastes like a cannoli doughnut. Needless to say, it's heavenly.

MAKES
12 pastries

1 recipe Brioche Dolce (page 240)

FILLING

8 ounces whole-milk ricotta

2 tablespoons mascarpone

¼ to ½ cup confectioners' sugar, to taste

½ teaspoon vanilla paste or pure vanilla extract

Zest of 1 orange

½ cup mini chocolate chips

ASSEMBLY

½ cup plain breadcrumbs

1 large egg, beaten

4 cups neutral oil, such as canola or grapeseed, for frying

- Prepare the brioche dough according to the instructions on page 240.

- WHILE THE DOUGH IS RISING, MAKE THE FILLING: In a medium bowl, combine the ricotta, mascarpone, confectioners' sugar, vanilla, orange zest, and chocolate chips and stir. Cover with plastic wrap and refrigerate until ready to bake.

- Line a baking sheet with parchment. After the first rise, remove the dough from the bowl and divide into 12 equal-size balls, rolling them as you go. Place the dough balls on the prepared baking sheet, leaving 2 inches between each one. Cover with a kitchen towel and set in a warm spot to proof for 1 hour, until almost doubled in size.

- On a floured work surface, flatten each dough ball, pressing the edges out with your fingers, allowing the center to remain a bit puffed.

- Place 1 teaspoon of the filling in the center of the dough. Lift the edges up around the filling, sealing them into the top of the dough. Gently reshape the dough into a ball, ensuring there are no holes. Return the iris to the baking sheet.

- Pour the breadcrumbs into a shallow dish. Add 1 tablespoon water to the beaten egg and, holding each ball in the palm of your hand, brush egg wash all over the dough and gently roll it in the breadcrumbs to cover.

- In a medium Dutch oven, heat the oil over medium-high heat until it reaches 350°F on a candy or deep-fry thermometer. Line a baking sheet with paper towels. Carefully drop 2 or 3 irises into the hot oil and fry for 3 minutes, until puffed, then flip and continue frying until puffed and deep golden brown all over, 2 to 3 minutes more. Use a slotted spoon to transfer them to the prepared baking sheet and repeat with the remaining irises. Serve immediately.

The Rizzuola

FRIED MEAT DOUGHNUTS

Here, the preparation is exactly same as the Iris (page 243), however, instead of cannoli cream, this is stuffed with savory ragù. Yes, a meaty doughnut, and it's marvelous. It's the same filling used in Sicilian Arancine (page 212): tomato sauce, ground beef, and peas. The *rosticcerie* also offer a "lighter" baked version called the *ravazzata*.

MAKES
12 doughnuts

1 recipe Brioche Salato (page 241)

FILLING

1 tablespoon extra-virgin olive oil

1 garlic clove, minced

½ cup chopped white onion

1 small carrot, finely chopped

½ pound 90% lean ground beef

1 cup canned tomato sauce

¼ cup canned small peas (I like Le Sueur)

1 large egg, beaten with 1 tablespoon water, for egg wash

• Prepare the brioche dough according to the instructions on page 241.

• WHILE THE DOUGH IS RISING, MAKE THE FILLING: In a medium saucepan, heat the oil over medium heat. Add the garlic, onion, and carrot and cook for 5 minutes, until the garlic is soft, and the onion is translucent.

• Add the beef and break it up with a wooden spoon, stirring to combine with the vegetables. Cook for 5 minutes, until the meat is no longer pink. Add the tomato sauce and stir to combine. Raise the heat to high to bring the sauce to a boil, then reduce the heat to maintain a simmer and cook for 10 minutes. Stir in the peas. Remove from the heat and set the filling aside to cool completely. (The filling can be made a day ahead and refrigerated until ready to use.)

• Line a baking sheet with parchment paper. Remove the dough from the bowl and divide into 12 equal-size balls, rolling them as you go. Set the dough balls on the baking sheet, leaving 2 inches between each. Cover with a kitchen towel and set in a warm spot to rise for 1 hour, until almost doubled in size.

• On a floured work surface, flatten each dough ball, pressing the edges out with your fingers, allowing the center to remain a bit puffed.

• Place 1 tablespoon of the filling in the center of the dough. Lift the edges up around the filling, sealing them into the top of the dough. Gently reshape the dough into a ball, ensuring there are no holes. Return the filled dough balls to the baking sheet, cover with a kitchen towel, and set in a warm spot to proof for 15 minutes.

• Holding each ball in the palm of your hand, brush all over with the egg wash and set them back on the baking sheet.

• In a medium Dutch oven, heat the neutral oil over medium-high heat until it reaches 350°F on a candy or deep-fry thermometer. Line a baking sheet with paper towels.

◆ Carefully drop two or three of the stuffed dough balls into the hot oil and cook for 2 to 3 minutes, until puffed, then flip and fry until puffed and deep golden brown all over, 2 to 3 minutes more. Use a slotted spoon to transfer them to the prepared baking sheet and repeat with the remaining dough balls. Serve immediately.

Danubio Salato

SAVORY PULL-APART ROLLS

The word *salato* in Italian means "salty." However, when used to describe a particular dish, it means "savory." Danubio is a Neapolitan pull-apart bread prepared either salato or dolce (sweet). After kneading a cheesy brioche dough, pieces are pinched off and rolled into equal-size balls. The balls are stuffed with cheese and ham and then arranged in a round baking dish for another rise. Once baked, it's a hands-on dish, where everyone can grab a roll and enjoy that melted center. To make the dolce version, omit the Parmigiano mixed into the dough and stuff the bread with pastry cream, chocolate, or a jam of your choosing. Whether dolce or salato, this bread is beautiful and great for crowds—and an excellent addition to the holiday table.

MAKES
one 11-inch round loaf; serves 8 to 10

1 recipe Brioche Salato (page 241)

FILLING

1 pound whole-milk mozzarella cheese, cut into 1-inch cubes

½ pound thinly sliced deli ham, cut into ½-inch squares

TOPPING

3 tablespoons extra-virgin olive oil

3 garlic cloves, peeled and smashed

1 teaspoon kosher salt

1 tablespoon poppy seeds

- Prepare the brioche dough according to the instructions on page 241.

- WHILE THE DOUGH IS RISING, MAKE THE FILLING: In a small saucepan, heat the oil on medium heat. Add the garlic and salt and cook for 3 minutes, until the garlic is soft and dark brown but not burned. Place a fine-mesh sieve over a heatproof bowl and strain the oil into it, discarding the garlic. Set the garlic oil aside.

- When the dough has risen, cut it into two equal pieces. Roll each piece into a 16-inch-long log, then cut each log into ten equal pieces, about 1½ ounces each. Press each piece into a flat circle.

RECIPE CONTINUES

- Take 2 or 3 pieces of mozzarella and a tablespoon of ham pieces and place them in the middle of the flattened piece of dough. Wrap the dough around the meat and cheese, pinching it closed while rolling it between your palms.

- Grease an 11-inch round baking dish or tart pan and arrange the dough balls in it in a circular pattern. Place the tart pan on a baking sheet. Cover with plastic wrap and set in a warm spot to proof for 30 minutes.

- Preheat the oven to 400°F.

- Brush the dough with the garlic oil and sprinkle with the poppy seeds. Bake for 10 minutes, then reduce the oven temperature to 350°F and bake for 30 to 35 minutes more, until the tops are lightly golden. Let cool for 5 minutes, then pull apart and enjoy.

Rollò con Wurstel

BRIOCHE-WRAPPED HOT DOGS

We're still using our versatile savory brioche dough, however, this time, instead of a fried stuffed bun, we are wrapping it around a hot dog and baking it up for a corded, bread-covered hot dog. They are egg washed and covered in sesame seeds, which, funny enough, reminds me of American hamburger buns. The hot dog warms and puffs in the oven, oozing its juices into the dough. I could eat these all day, every day.

MAKES
12 baked hot dogs

1 recipe Brioche Salato (page 241)

12 hot dogs

1 large egg, beaten

1 tablespoon sesame seeds

2 teaspoons kosher salt

◆ Prepare the brioche dough according to the instructions on page 241.

◆ While the dough is rising, line a baking sheet with parchment paper. Remove the dough from the bowl and divide it into 12 equal-size balls, rolling them as you go. Place the dough balls on the prepared baking sheet, leaving 2 inches between each one. Cover with a kitchen towel and set in a warm spot to rise for 1 hour, until almost doubled in size.

◆ Roll each ball into a long cord, about 16 inches long. Holding the hot dog, press one end of the dough into the end of the hot dog and wrap it around the hot dog until it reaches the other end.

◆ Return the wrapped hot dogs to the baking sheet, cover with a kitchen towel, and set in a warm spot to proof for 15 minutes.

◆ While the dough is proofing, set an oven rack in the middle position and preheat the oven to 350°F.

◆ Mix the beaten egg with 1 tablespoon water and brush it over the tops of each rolled hot dog. Sprinkle with the sesame seeds and salt.

◆ Bake for 15 minutes. Move the baking sheet to the top rack and bake for 10 minutes more. Serve immediately or at room temperature.

ROLLÒ CON WURSTEL, PAGE 249

Gelato con Brioche

BRIOCHE ICE CREAM SANDWICHES

The Italian ice cream sandwich! Sicilian ice cream shops offer this option alongside cones and cups. Golden brown brioche rolls are baked with a small ball of dough on top known as a *tuppo* (Italian for "bun," a reference to the traditional hairstyle of Sicilian nonnas), then stuffed with gelato. I love eating gelato this way with a generous amount of whipped cream. The *brioche col tuppo* can also be served alongside granita (see page 141) for dipping into the granita before eating.

MAKES
12 brioche buns

1 recipe Brioche Dolce (page 240; increase the eggs to 3, and the butter to 8 tablespoons/113 grams)

¼ cup (56 grams) heavy cream

1 tablespoon confectioners' sugar

Pinch of kosher salt

2 pints gelato

Whipped cream, for serving

- Prepare the brioche dough according to the instructions on page 240.
- While the dough is rising, line a baking sheet with parchment paper. Remove the dough from the bowl and divide into 12 equal-size balls. Pinch off a small piece of dough (10 grams) from each ball and roll into a small ball. Place the large dough balls on the prepared baking sheet, leaving 2 inches between each one. Make a small dimple in the top of each large ball and place the small balls of dough in the dimples (this is the "tuppo"). Cover with a kitchen towel and set in a warm spot to proof for 1 hour, until almost doubled in size.
- During the last 20 minutes of the proof, preheat the oven to 350°F.
- In a small bowl, whisk the cream, confectioners' sugar, and salt to make a glaze.
- Brush the glaze all over the dough and place in the oven. Bake for 25 minutes, until the tops begin to brown. Let cool completely.
- Cut each brioche roll in half horizontally and place a scoop of gelato on the bottom half. Press the top of the roll over the gelato and serve with a dollop of whipped cream.

LA CUCINA ITALIANA
The Italian Kitchen

AS A FULL-TIME recipe developer and cookbook author, I always have a fully stocked pantry. I dislike running to the grocery store for one ingredient and love a good deal, so if something I use regularly is on sale, I'll pick up a few extras. Having what you need at your fingertips when it's time to cook or bake is a game changer. If the cupboards are bare, and a snack attack hits, you will most likely eat something unhealthy and processed—which is okay every once in a while, but not great on the daily. This section will set you up to be a master (and prepared) *spuntini* creator.

Along with my pantry staples, I've included recipes I make in bulk and stock in the freezer. Then, on days when work or life's mishaps put my day into fast-forward mode, I am not stuck with nothing to serve for dinner. The same practice applies to snacking. Whether it's your midmorning snack after a big workout, the 4 p.m. hungry-kid stampede after school, or a few friends dropping by for drinks, these ingredients will be your arsenal of delicious snack building blocks.

Pantry & Fridge

AMARENA CHERRIES / MARASCHINO CHERRIES

Amarena cherries are the best-preserved cherries you can buy. I love the flavor and use them in desserts and cocktails. Fabbri brand Amarenas can be found in a pretty white jar with blue decorations. Maraschinos are okay as a substitute, so feel free to use them instead if you can't source Amarenas.

COFFEE

Italians love coffee, and good-quality beans to brew espresso are a must-have. Invest in a proper espresso machine, too, if you can, or get an old-school stovetop espresso maker—it makes a respectable espresso for a lot less than one of the fancier machines.

DRIED OREGANO

My grandfather loved oregano. He would pick a bunch of it on his way home from work and hang the branches upside down in his woodworking shed so when you walked in, it smelled like wood shavings and oregano. I love dried oregano and I put it in everything. I use the wooden spoons my grandfather made me to stir my pasta and when I crush the oregano in my palms, I immediately think of my beloved nonno.

OO FLOUR

This finely milled wheat flour is really the all-purpose flour of Italy. Italians use it for pizza and baking *a lot*. I have gotten so accustomed to developing recipes with it that it has become my go-to flour. One of the things I love about it is that it can withstand high baking temperatures, which is perfect for a charred pizza crust and great for any recipe that requires a dough or delicate crust.

GOOD BREAD

Having good bread on hand means a delicious snack is always right at your fingertips. It's a vehicle for jams, spreads, pâtés, and a lovely caponata. Toasted, crostini-style, is always my favorite way to serve it.

HIGH-QUALITY EXTRA-VIRGIN OLIVE OIL

As a Southern Italian, I was raised on good extra-virgin olive oil. We joke that the only reason my mother bought butter was for our toast in the morning. We cook, fry, and bake with it. For deep-frying, I turn to canola or grapeseed oil, but otherwise, I stick with a fruity EVOO and buy it on the regular. I do not like "light" olive oil, so for my baking recipes, just use the best olive oil you can afford.

HOMEMADE CONDIMENTS

The mixes and spreads on pages 156–162 come together quickly, can live safely in an airtight container in the fridge for a week or more, and are great to have on hand for tramezzini fillings.

HONEY

A delicious, natural sweetener that I use for sweets and drizzles. My favorite is Italian acacia honey. Brezzo makes a fine product.

LATTE DI MANDORLE / ALMOND MILK

Latte di mandorle translates to "almond milk." In Italy, however, this refers to two different products. The first, almond milk, is the dairy substitute beverage many of us stir into our coffee. However, there is also a specialty product with the same name. It is an opaque white, sweetened condensed syrup used in coffees and as a drink for children. When I was a child, my parents would bring it home from Italy and pour it into a tall glass with ice and water. A quick stir, and it became a sweet almond drink I loved. This version is excellent in cocktails and served in coffees as a sweetener and flavor enhancer and can be found in Italian specialty shops and delis.

LEMONS AND ORANGES

Lemon and orange zest and juice are constants in Italian desserts. As Italians do not use a lot of sugar in their confections, they rely on other flavors like citrus to bring out the sweetness of doughs and fillings. Citrus also works well in savory dishes.

MEATS AND CHEESE

'Nduja, prosciutto, deli ham (prosciutto cotto), pancetta, soppressata, Parmigiano Reggiano, Pecorino Romano, and ricotta are used as ingredients in many, many spuntini, but they also build a wonderful antipasto platter on their own. In my opinion, there should always be hunks of pecorino and Parmigiano in the fridge. The rinds should be saved and added to soups and tomato sauce for an extra boost of flavor, too.

NUTS

I'm nuts about nuts. Always have been. And Italians put them in everything! Pine nuts, almonds, hazelnuts, and pistachios are big stars in both sweet and savory dishes. I also love making Noci Croccante (see page 260), a delicious Italian brittle. I serve it as a lovely sweet snack for guests to nibble on, but it's also the perfect topping for my Panna Cotta (page 126) and Torta Tenerina (page 93), crumbled over whipped cream before serving. It even tastes great on gelato.

OILY FISH

Anchovies and tuna packed in oil are Italian pantry staples. Eaten on their own, with bread, or in pizza and pasta, jarred or tinned fish can assist in producing a meal in minutes. If you can't find tuna in oil, buy water-packed tuna and add oil, but the flavor of the tuna in oil is so much better.

OLIVES AND CAPERS

Olives and capers provide punch and brine to whatever food they touch. They are produced throughout Italy and are used in numerous applications, like fillers, sauces, spreads, and flavor bombs. They also keep forever in the pantry or fridge (after opening) so I am never without!

TOMATO SAUCES

There are two tomato sauce recipes I use in my home: my mother's slow-cooked sauce (see page 264) and a quick marinara sauce (see page 265). Either will work for any recipe in this book that calls for tomato sauce.

VANILLA LEAVENER / VANILLA POWDER

Lievito Bertolini is a fantastic product used by Italian bakers and home cooks to make cakes and cookies. It's a commercial product, packed in little envelopes, and it's a combination of baking powder and vanilla powder. Paneangeli is another widely used brand name. You can find them on Amazon, but I created a homemade version by combining vanilla powder and baking powder (see Note, page 46).

Vanilla powder is relatively easy to source via Amazon or dedicated spice stores, and I prefer it to extract in doughs and cakes. Extract can be substituted, but I encourage you to give it a try, it's wonderful. The powder imparts a sweet and delicate scent to the dry ingredients that you can still smell when you bite into the finished dessert.

The Bar

Sweet liqueurs are used as another flavor enhancer in desserts, and Italians are also willing to drop a bit into their afternoon espresso! Building a well-stocked bar of Italian liquor will allow you to have an aperitivo ready when *apericena* hits. Along with these staples, it's always smart to have a few of your favorite white and red wines on hand as well.

Some of my must-haves are:

Amaretto
Aperol
Campari
Frangelico
Gin
Grappa
Limoncello
Marsala
Prosecco
Rum
Sambuca
Soda water
Sparkling rosé
Sweet vermouth
Triple sec
Vermouth rosso

NOCI CROCCANTE (NUT BRITTLE)

My mother makes this homemade candy as a holiday snack, and it always has a place on the Christmas cookie trays that we gift to friends and family. The baking soda reacts with the sugar and creates little pockets of air, giving the candy a great snap. I use hazelnuts because they are my favorite, but feel free to sub almonds, walnuts, or a combination of the three. I always add orange zest, too, for a bit of warmth.

Makes one 13 × 18-inch pan; serves 12

3 tablespoons unsalted butter, cut into 1-inch cubes, plus more for greasing

1¾ cups sugar

1 cup light corn syrup

Zest of 1 orange

½ teaspoon kosher salt

2¼ cups blanched hazelnuts, toasted and chopped

1 teaspoon pure vanilla extract

1 teaspoon baking soda

Line a 13 × 18-inch baking sheet with parchment paper and grease the parchment with butter.

Attach a candy thermometer to the side of a medium pot. Pour 1 cup water, the sugar, corn syrup, orange zest, and salt into the pot and heat over medium heat, stirring, until the ingredients are fully incorporated. Raise the heat to medium-high and cook until the mixture reaches 320°F. Reduce the heat to low and cook, stirring occasionally with a wooden spoon, until golden brown in color, about 20 minutes.

Working quickly, drop in the cubed butter and stir a few times to incorporate. Add the nuts, vanilla, and baking soda and stir to coat the nuts completely in the syrup. Be careful—the mixture will bubble up while stirring and become the color of a creamy honey. Remove the pot from the heat and pour the mixture onto the prepared baking sheet, spreading it into a thin, even layer. Let stand until the brittle is firm and completely cooled, about 5 minutes, then break into shards.

Store in an airtight container or freezer bags at room temperature for up to 1 month.

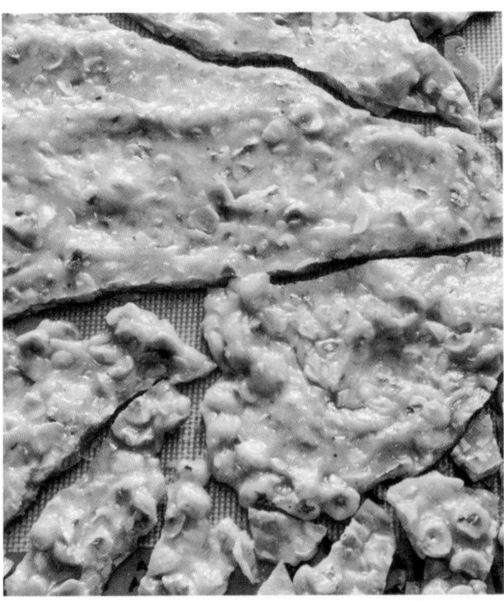

CHOCOLATE-HAZELNUT SPREAD

Growing up in an Italian American household, we didn't have a lot of processed foods in the pantry. My mother didn't buy them, so I wasn't used to a cabinet full of packaged snacks. However, one item I could always count on was Nutella. It was our alternative to peanut butter. After a long day at school, I'd drop my backpack, grab a butter knife, and spread a generous amount of the chocolate nut spread on some bread.

Today, in a more health-conscious world, processed foods are something, when possible, we try to avoid in my house. So when my friend Lisetta gave me her recipe for homemade Nutella, I was elated. Not only is it void of palm oil and soy, but you can also control the amount of sugar and the ratio of milk to dark chocolate. Italians love Nutella, hence, chocolate-hazelnut spread is an ingredient in several recipes in this book. You can certainly use Nutella out of a jar, but give this homemade version a try.

Makes 3 cups

1½ cups (205 grams) hazelnuts

½ cup (100 grams) granulated sugar

6 ounces (170 grams) high-quality milk chocolate

6 ounces (170 grams) high-quality dark chocolate, preferably 70% cacao

1 cup (227 grams) whole milk

2 tablespoons hazelnut oil

Preheat the oven to 350°F.

Place the hazelnuts on a rimmed baking sheet and toast in the oven until fragrant and golden brown, 7 to 10 minutes.

While the hazelnuts are toasting, in a small saucepan, combine the sugar, milk chocolate, dark chocolate, and milk and heat over low heat until the chocolate has completely melted.

Let the toasted hazelnuts cool for 10 minutes. Add them to a food processor and grind until they turn into a paste, similar to nut butter. Add the chocolate mixture to the food processor and pulse a few times to combine. With the motor running, slowly add the hazelnut oil and process until fully combined. Store the spread in an airtight container in the refrigerator for up to 1 week.

ALL-PURPOSE PIZZA DOUGH

One dough, so many possibilities!

My dough recipes came about through lots of trial and error. This one will not only create a tasty pizza, it can also be used for a number of other delicious snacks, like the Girelle on page 231. This dough is ready for use one hour after making, as it needs only a rise followed a good punching down before use. However, if you have the time, let it spend the night in the fridge.

Makes two 12-inch pizzas

1¼ cups (300 grams) warm water (110°F)

1 (¼-ounce) packet active dry yeast (2¼ teaspoons)

2 teaspoons sugar

3½ cups (406 grams) 00 flour, plus more for dusting

1 teaspoon kosher salt

2 tablespoons extra-virgin olive oil

In a small bowl, whisk together the water, yeast, and sugar. Let stand for 5 minutes.

In the bowl of a stand mixer fitted with the dough hook, combine the flour and salt. With the motor running on low speed, slowly add the yeast mixture and mix until a slightly wet dough forms. (Alternatively, in a large bowl, stir the dough ingredients together by hand.)

Transfer the dough to a floured work surface and form it into a ball. If the dough is tacky, add just enough flour to pull at the ends and bring them to the center until the surface is smooth. The dough should be very soft and supple but dry to the touch.

Place the dough in a large bowl and drizzle the oil on top. Spread the oil over the surface of the dough and cover the top of the bowl tightly with plastic wrap so it is completely sealed. Place the bowl in a warm spot for 1 hour or until it has doubled in size (see Note).

Once the dough has risen, remove it from the bowl and cover it with the plastic wrap until ready to use. If you are using it immediately, place it directly onto a baking sheet (pick a pizza recipe and go!). If using it later, refrigerate it.

If you have the time, refrigerating the wrapped dough overnight will give you optimal results. Allow the dough to come to room temperature before stretching it into your desired pizza shape.

NOTE

Try leavening the dough in the microwave. Run your microwave (empty) on high for 2 minutes. Place the dough inside and shut the door. This creates a nice proofing environment.

OLIVE CONDITE

Olive condite is a simple marinated olive recipe that uses a garlic-infused oil to enhance the flavor of the olives. Serve them in a small dish alongside your favorite predinner drinks.

Makes 2 cups

- ¾ cup extra-virgin olive oil
- 1 lemon, zested into large strips
- 1 orange, zested into large strips
- ½ teaspoon crushed red pepper flakes
- 3 garlic cloves, peeled and lightly smashed
- 2 or 3 oregano sprigs
- 2 cups mixed olives
- Kosher salt and freshly ground black pepper

In a medium saucepan, heat the olive oil over low heat. Add the zests, red pepper flakes, and garlic. Once the oil begins to bubble, reduce the heat to low, add the oregano, and simmer for 5 to 7 minutes. When the citrus peels and garlic just begin to turn golden, remove from the heat and cover the pot. Let stand for 10 to 15 minutes.

Place the olives in a medium bowl and pour the infused oil over them. Pick out the oregano stems. Toss to coat and season to taste. They can be served warm or at room temperature. If not serving immediately, transfer the olives and oil to a jar, cover, and set aside at room temperature, or refrigerate overnight. Remove 1 hour before serving to bring to room temperature. To serve, remove the olives from the jar with a slotted spoon.

GINA'S TOMATO SAUCE

This is my mother's slow-cooked sauce, my "Sunday Sauce." I make it in large quantities and freeze it in quart containers, so I have it on hand for the many recipes I use it in. I also freeze it in pint containers for when I need it for pizza topping or a dipping sauce.

Makes 7 cups

- ½ cup extra-virgin olive oil
- 4 or 5 fresh basil leaves, plus 1 tablespoon chopped fresh basil
- 2 garlic cloves, peeled and lightly smashed
- 1 teaspoon crushed red pepper flakes (optional)
- 2 (28-ounce) cans crushed tomatoes
- Kosher salt and freshly ground black pepper

In a small skillet, combine the oil, basil leaves, garlic, and red pepper flakes (if using). Heat over low heat for 10 to 15 minutes, until the basil is toasted and the garlic is golden brown. Remove from the heat. Use a slotted spoon to remove and discard the basil and garlic.

In a large saucepan, heat the crushed tomatoes over medium heat. Season with salt and black pepper, add the infused olive oil, and stir to combine. Raise the heat to medium-high to bring the mixture to a boil, then immediately reduce the heat to low and simmer for 45 minutes. Remove from the heat, toss in the chopped basil, and stir to combine. Let cool to room temperature before transferring to storage containers. The sauce will keep in the refrigerator for up to 1 week or in the freezer for up to 1 month.

QUICK MARINARA SAUCE

My mother's slow-cooked sauce (see page 264) takes a bit of planning, so if I don't have the time or I'm out of my freezer stock, I make this quick version.

Makes 2½ cups

- ¼ cup extra-virgin olive oil
- 2 garlic cloves, peeled and lightly smashed
- Pinch of crushed red pepper flakes (optional)
- 3 fresh basil leaves
- 1 (24.5-ounce) jar tomato passata (I love Mutti)
- 2 teaspoons kosher salt
- 2 teaspoons dried oregano

In a medium saucepan, heat the oil over medium-low heat. Add the garlic cloves, red pepper flakes (if using), and basil leaves and cook for 4 to 5 minutes, until the garlic is a dark brown. Remove the infused oil from the heat. Use a slotted spoon to remove and discard the garlic and basil. Let the oil cool for a minute or so, then add the tomato passata, salt, and oregano. Stir to combine.

Warm the sauce over low heat and simmer for 25 minutes. Remove from the heat and allow to cool to room temperature before transferring to airtight containers for storage. The sauce will keep in the refrigerator for up to 1 week or in the freezer for up to 1 month.

PICKLED RED ONIONS

Great in sandwiches or on salads, these onions add a nice punch of acid and texture.

Makes 4 cups

- 2 cups red wine vinegar
- 2 tablespoons sugar
- 2 tablespoons kosher salt
- 2 red onions, thinly sliced
- 2 garlic cloves, peeled and lightly smashed
- 1 teaspoon whole black peppercorns

In a medium saucepan, combine the vinegar, sugar, salt, and 1 cup water. Bring to a boil over high heat and stir until the sugar and salt have dissolved. Remove from the heat.

Stir in the onions, garlic, and peppercorns and let cool to room temperature. Pour the mixture into a 10- to 16-ounce glass jar and cover with a tight-fitting lid. Allow the onions to pickle for at least 2 hours or preferably overnight before using. They will keep in the refrigerator for up to 2 weeks.

ITALIAN AIOLI

This aioli is great spread on sandwiches or served as a dipping sauce for Polpette di Tonno (page 185). It comes together in minutes with an immersion blender.

Makes ¾ cup

- 1 large egg yolk
- Zest of 1 lemon
- 1 tablespoon fresh lemon juice
- 1½ teaspoons white wine vinegar
- About ½ cup extra-virgin olive oil
- Kosher salt and freshly ground black pepper

In a small food processor, combine the egg, lemon zest and juice, and vinegar and pulse to combine (alternatively, combine the ingredients in a wide-mouthed 1-pint jar and pulse with an immersion blender). With the motor running, slowly stream in the oil until the aioli begins to thicken. Season with salt and pepper.

Store in an airtight container in the refrigerator for up to 1 week.

PERFECT PESTO

One of my favorite pasta toppings, pesto is one of Italy's most versatile sauces. Slather it on a sandwich or spread a thin layer of it on crostini and pizza crust.

Makes 4 cups

- 5½ cups fresh basil leaves, cleaned and towel-dried
- 1 cup grated Parmigiano Reggiano cheese
- 5 garlic cloves, peeled
- 2 teaspoons kosher salt
- 1½ cups extra-virgin olive oil, plus more for storing
- ½ cup pine nuts

In a food processor, pulse the basil, cheese, garlic, and salt. Then, with the motor running, slowly stream in the oil and process until a thick paste forms.

If not serving immediately, transfer the pesto to an airtight container and pour a thin layer of oil on top to prevent oxidation, then cover. Refrigerate for up to 1 week or freeze for up to 1 month.

When ready to use, toast the pine nuts in a dry pan over medium heat for 5 minutes and fold them into the pesto.

CHEESY BREADCRUMBS

I hate waste! So, many years ago, when it became apparent that my children would not eat the *culo* (butt) of the sandwich bread loaves, I knew I had to find something to do with them. These breadcrumbs were the answer.

Breadcrumbs are used a lot in Italian cooking—and throughout this book—as a coating, filler, or topping. I use a lot of breadcrumbs! Yes, you can buy premade crumbs from the store, but I promise these are much, much better.

Makes 3½ cups

- 8 slices white sandwich bread, preferably the ends
- 2 tablespoons extra-virgin olive oil
- 1 teaspoon kosher salt
- 1 teaspoon dried oregano
- ½ cup grated Pecorino Romano cheese

Preheat the oven to 350°F.

Place the bread on a baking sheet in a single layer and drizzle with the oil. Bake for 10 minutes, until the bread is toasted and brown. Remove from the oven and let cool completely.

In a food processor, pulse the bread to break it up into fine crumbs (a few bigger bits are fine). Add the salt, oregano, and cheese and pulse until fully combined. Store in an airtight container in the refrigerator for up to 3 weeks.

ACKNOWLEDGMENTS

First and foremost, thank you to my loving, supportive family:

Phil, with your support, I cook all day, do what I love most, and investigate, develop, and celebrate food.

Alessandra, Veronica, and Dante, everything I do, I do for you. You are the bright lights of my life.

To my parents, whose unwavering support, love, and belief in me have given me the courage to charge ahead and continue making this dream a reality.

To the DeCrosta family. To my sister, Luciana—you are my extraordinary compass in life, now and forever. Gigi and Maxie, Teetee loves you and will always have a fully stocked pantry for the car ride home. Thank you, Chris, for all that you have done for me.

This book was just an idea until Sarah Smith made it a reality. Thank you, Sarah, for treating your clients like dear friends and constantly cheerleading from the sidelines. When inspiration hits, you are my first call.

To Kim Yorio: You are a guiding light and a support system. You work hard and you care even harder. Thank you for being you.

To Spuntini Squadra USA: Linda Xiao, Maeve Sheridan, Greg Lofts, and Maya Rucker. Our photo shoot was a well-oiled machine from the beginning until the final shot. Thank you for taking so much care to make this book something I am so very proud to present to the world. And to Greg, an extra shout-out for the use of those gorgeous hands, both in the test kitchen and on set.

To Spuntini Squadra Italia: Colgo l'opportunità per ringraziare Andrea Di Lorenzo, Giovanna Di Lisciandro e Emanuele Di Cesare; Andrea in modo particolare per le straordinarie fotografie di tre città—Roma *caput mundi*, Napoli e Palermo—senza dubbio fra le più belle del mondo. Giovanna per la sua perizia nell'avermi fatto girare l'incantevole Palermo. Emanuele per aver condiviso la sua conoscenza da *insider* di Napoli.

È stata mia fortuna—non solo professionale, ma anche personale—averli conosciuti. Ringrazio in modo particolare Mauro Pala per avermi dato generosamente del suo tempo e per avermi gentilissimamente fatto capire il perché del suo amore per una squisita cittadina, la "sua" Cagliari.

To Amanda Englander: Thank you for understanding this concept and my deep obsession with Italian food. Your enthusiasm, advice, and direction gave me the tools to create this delicious love letter to my homeland.

To Caitlin Leffel: Thank you for being the dream editor who understands la dolce vita and my passion to get it right every.single. time. Your expertise and love of all things Italian made this not only the most productive partnership, but also just so much fun. Grazie mille cara.

To the Union Square team, Lisa Forde, Jennifer Halper, and Blanca Oliviery. Thank you for your work and dedication.

To uber-talented designer Laura Palese: You once again swooped in and made my vision the most beautiful reality. For the second time in my bookmaking biz, you have created something beyond my wildest dreams.

To Alexandra Utter, who will stop her hectic life to test my recipes immediately.

To Laura Arnold: Thank you for your diligent testing. Your feedback was critical.

INDEX

Note: Page references in *italics* indicate recipe photographs.